Checking INN

Checking INN

The Adventures of a Tour Director

Herb Reisenfeld

ORANGE *frazer* PRESS

Wilmington, Ohio

ISBN 978-1939710-529
Copyright©2016 Herb Reisenfeld

Published by:
Orange Frazer Press
P.O. Box 214
Wilmington, OH 45177
Telephone: 937.382.3196 for price and shipping information.
Website: www.orangefrazer.com

Cover illustration: Donald Wymore

Book and cover design: Alyson Rua and Orange Frazer Press

Library of Congress Control Number: 2016951323

First Printing

To our fantastic, wonderful,
devoted daughter, Julianne

In Memory

Susan Jane Reisenfeld—Loving Wife

Steven B. Reisenfeld—Courageous Son

Sylvan P. Reisenfeld—Brother and Best Friend

Nancy J. Farasey—Fun Loving Sister-in-Law

David and Sarah Reisenfeld—Wonderful Parents

Barney and Ruby Wright Rapp—Outstanding In-Laws

Contents

Introduction ix

The Early Years I

Love at First Sight 5

My Second Home 6

Red Rooters Club I0

Into the Fire I2

Play Ball I9

Extra Innings 2I

The Machine Years 23

Over There 26

Celebrities 29

Swiss Miss 32

Funny Incidents 35

Rosemary 37

Ship Tales 4I

Lost and Found 47

White Suit 55

Get Out the Brooms 57

Waite-ing for the Rain 59

Who's on Deck 6I

The Rough Riders.................................... 67

Show Business....................................... 70

Round and Round We Go........................ 71

Hell No, We Won't Go 74

Lemons... 77

You Won't Believe This 79

The Weather Outside is Frightful 85

We Paid for It.. 87

Don't Jump.. 88

What's Poppin'....................................... 90

Hold On 92

Baby It's Cold Inside 95

Bing-Bang 97

Weekend Warriors 98

Don't Miss the Boat............................... 101

Surprise Package.................................... 104

We Have Cooties.................................... 107

The Hall.. 109

Rubbing Elbows 113

Foreign Relations................................... 115

Civil-Liberty 121

Borscht 124

Showtime... 127

Favorites 129

Chuckles 133

Not Finished.. 140

About the Author 143

Introduction

It started when I was eight years old. My interest for amazing places and mystifying locations was ignited. Three significant moments inspired me to want to tour the world and to see all it had to show me.

First, I remember the excitement of my Uncle Sam returning home after being in WWII. He had served under General Patton as a radio operator in England, Italy, and France. During his visit with us, he spoke of the places he visited: the cities, towns, and the people. My uncle had come to America with my father from Poland when they were very young men. And now, he had returned to Europe as an American soldier twenty years later.

He gave me a pewter piece that was oval shaped and had a miniature Eiffel Tower and the Arc de Triomphe attached to it. I held this item often and looked at the two objects, amazed at both of these structures.

The next thing that piqued my interest was the history of my father and grandparents. As immigrants and later naturalized American citizens, they had emigrated from Eastern Europe. As mentioned, my father came from Poland in 1920 and had sisters and a brother who preceded him to America. Later, he helped to bring another sister and his mother and father to America. One sister, her husband, and their two children were murdered in the Holocaust. My mother was born in Newport, Kentucky, the first in her family to be born an American. Her parents were from Russia and came to America via London, having lived there several years before arriving in Cincinnati. They all left their homeland to escape the oppression they constantly faced. While they mostly came from small villages, I was fascinated by the stories they told of their homeland; and, in my mind, I imagined where and how they lived and wanted some day to visit those places.

Finally, a book was gifted to my brother Sylvan entitled *Marvels of the World*, written by Richard Halliburton. This book contained pictures of natural sites, building, and monuments. Included were pictures of the Taj Mahal and the Empire State Building (with a depiction of a dirigible attached to the top mast of the building as this was an original conception), and many more exotic places.

As a young boy growing up in the Cincinnati suburb of Price Hill, I was fascinated with the pictures of wondrous places. I fantasized flying off to exotic parts of the world. Every day I would gaze at the black and white photographs and think how different the world is compared to where we were living.

Eventually the *Marvels of the World* book became mine and I kept it on my bookshelf, constantly thumbing through it and imagining, through the eyes of a young child, the adventures that I would have growing up to be a world traveler.

After sixty-nine years, I still have that well-worn book. It opened my mind and imagination to all the incredible places that I wanted to visit. This was long before I heard the term "Bucket List." Fortunately, I have had the opportunity to visit many of those places and still have the longing to see much more, because of course, most of my working career *has* been in travel.

Checking Inn shares the adventures and stories that remain etched in my memory from forty-three years in the travel industry. You can't make these stories up! They helped to shape my life and have taken me on unbelievable journeys. Enjoy reading these adventures. They're all true!

Checking INN

The Early Years

Though the magic of travel adventures thrilled me throughout my youth, I was also interested in other things. While attending grade school at Carson Elementary, I found my main interest was in sports. I participated in track, but my core sport was baseball. My dad, Dave Reisenfeld, arrived in America at the age of sixteen with his younger brother Sam. Dad immediately fell in love with America's pastime—baseball. He visited his sister who lived in the Bronx borough of New York City, just two blocks from Yankee Stadium. He saw the great Yankee team of the late 1920s and went to four straight games at the "House that Ruth Built." Later he moved to Cincinnati's West End and he and his brother learned the game, finally playing in a baseball league.

Growing up, my brother Syl and I, under the tutelage of our dad, became ardent Reds fans. Dad would tell us of the great Reds players he watched, especially Eddy Roush who was inducted into the National Baseball Hall of Fame. Every year we would go to Crosley Field on Opening Day and sit out in the bleachers. I can still visualize the temporary seats that were set up in the outfield to accommodate the large crowd. If a ball

Even at the tender age of two, Herb was ready to travel.

was hit into that area it was a ground rule double. I can still feel the cold as we sat bundled up in blankets to keep warm from the chill of a cold early April day. But, we loved going to the game and seeing our favorite players, most of whom would be there year after year.

My mother Sarah was the other person to make up our quartet. She was a terrific sport, putting up with three males who constantly talked and played baseball all year long. We even had a board game called "Rube Bressler's Baseball." There were little discs with the figure of a player and we would throw the dice when it was our turn to bat with the number determining the batter's success at the plate. We chose our teams and I hoped that my Reds would win our nine inning game. This game was our way to keep baseball alive until it was time again for spring training.

I started playing Knothole baseball when I was ten. My dad had a real estate brokerage that was our team sponsor and he managed teams for both Syl and me. My brother went on to play on the Western Hills High School team that won the Ohio state championship in 1950. Later he managed our Reisenfeld Realty class "A" team that was also very successful.

I was a left-handed pitcher who was blessed with a great fastball. However, as is the case with many southpaws, I didn't always know where the pitch was going and I would often, though not intentionally, hit the batter. When I had good control, I pitched several no-hitters. My reputation for being "wild" brought fear to many of the batters I faced. They were too scared to stand in the batter's box. On one occasion, when warming up at the start of a game at Dempsey Park, I wound up and the ball sailed over the backstop. This shook up the players and their parents. There was a lot of screaming going on. They were concerned for their boys, as they didn't know where my pitches might go. Truthfully, I wasn't always sure either, as I would wind up and cut loose. I still run into people who were there that night and they always remind me of the pitch that looked like a missile, directed into the stands behind the backstop. Oh, and in case you are wondering, I settled down and we won the game, even though the booing was quite loud.

Our team was chosen to play the first game at the dedication of Spinney Field. This was long before it became the Cincinnati Bengals practice field. The ceremony was officiated by Cincinnati Mayor Albert Cash. We played our rival team, Tony's Café, and it was so hot that they gave us cabbage leaves to put under our hats to reflect the heat. We lost the game 1–0 when they bunted and a man on third scored on a wild throw to the plate. I pitched a one-hitter and their pitcher pitched a no-hitter. Well, you can't win 'em all.

Love at First Sight

In 1953, our family moved to the Eastern suburb of Roselawn. This was highly unusual as West-Siders would never cross the viaduct and become East-Siders. It was not supposed to happen.

This is when my life really changed. I met the girl of my dreams that fall. The New Woodward High School opened on the corner of Reading Road and Seymour Avenue. I was new to this area and didn't know anyone as I entered the brand new building as a ninth-grade student. After a few weeks, I became friends with some of my classmates and was invited to come over to one of their homes on Beaverton Avenue. After hanging out there for a while, we walked down to the dead-end of the street to see if one of their neighbors, Susie Rapp, was home. We were told she was at a neighbor's house. When we finally tracked her down, I stopped in my tracks. I saw her and my heart melted. I knew I had to see her again.

A week later we met again, and again. I found out she was one of four daughters. She had three sisters Patty, Nancy, and Cindy. What I didn't know then is that she had famous parents. Her father was Barney Rapp and her mother was Ruby Wright.

My Second Home

I was just fifteen years old when I met Susie and I would ride my Schwinn bike over to her house. The Rapp home was always open to friends of their daughters, and there were a lot of friends. To this day, many talk about the wonderful memories of Ruby making cookies for everyone. Both she and Barney made everyone feel welcome and glad to be there.

Barney Rapp had an entertainment booking agency in the Gibson Hotel. In the 1930s and 40s he had a band called "Barney Rapp and his New Englanders." He was from New Haven, Connecticut, where his father was a men's tailor and made custom suits for well-to-do Yale University students. Barney had a nightclub in New Haven in an entertainment area called Savin Rock which began in the late 19th century as a regionally renowned seaside resort. A hurricane in 1938 destroyed his and most of the other buildings there. Barney went on the road with his band playing at theaters, universities, and clubs. His band even recorded for RCA Victor Records. They were very popular.

Barney was playing in New York City at a major hotel and his brother, who went by his professional name, Barry Wood, introduced him to a girl singer by the name of Ruby Wright. Barry was a vocalist on the radio show *Hit Parade* and later became a top executive with NBC, producing the *Bell Telephone Hour, Wide Wide World,* and later was in charge of NBC color television production.

Ruby had been a vocalist with the Jan Garber Orchestra and after meeting Barney, she became the band's vocalist and was known as the "Sweetheart of the Air."

A short time later they married and came to Cincinnati where they played extended engagements at the Gibson Hotel, Castle Farms, Lookout House, and other hot spots. They loved Cincinnati and decided to make it their home. They opened a nightclub in Bond Hill called The Sign of the Drum. Barney was the bandleader and Ruby was the featured vocalist.

In late 1939, Ruby became pregnant with their first child and had to give up performing at the club. Barney started auditioning girl singers and a friend of Barney's, Grace Raines, a vocal coach and talent director at WLW radio, brought a young girl to audition for Barney. Her name was Doris Kappelhoff and she got the job as the featured vocalist to replace Ruby.

After much success at the club, Barney told Doris that he wanted to advertise in the newspaper and put her name on the marquee, but her name wouldn't fit. He recommended that she change her name professionally and suggested that since she sang "Day After Day" which was popular with the patrons, that she change her name to Doris Day. History was made! Doris would end up marrying her first husband, Al Jordan, who was a trom-

Doris Day and Barney Rapp in the early 1950s.

bone player in Barney's band. He was the father of their son, Terry. Barney had a good ear for talent. He was also the first agent for Rosemary and Betty Clooney.

Ruby gave birth to their first daughter, Susie; and, perhaps if it wasn't for her mother being pregnant with her, there may have not been a girl named Doris Day. Ruby was from Anderson, Indiana. After graduating from high school, she and two friends formed a singing group which later led to Ruby becoming a lead vocalist with big bands.

Susie Rapp and I married in 1963 and almost made it to our 52nd anniversary. I lost my love in November 2015, after having known her for sixty-two years. She was an outstanding wife and mother!

Ruby and Barney were great in-laws and were wonderful to their fans and clients. They were a major part of Cincinnati's entertainment history and will long be remembered.

Red Rooters Club

As I mentioned, Barney Rapp was a band leader but he also was a booking agent for other musical acts and performers. Beyond that, he also produced Christmas shows for large Cincinnati companies and, for many years, produced the Syrian Shrine Circus.

Barney's booking office was in the Sinton Hotel, located at 4th and Vine streets. This hotel was also home of the radio station that broadcast the Cincinnati Reds games. The studio was near Barney's office and Waite Hoyt, the Reds broadcaster, would frequently see Barney. In the fall of 1956, the Reds were locked in a tight pennant race with the Milwaukee Braves. That was the year Ted Kluszewski, Wally Post, and Gus Bell were setting records hitting home runs.

Possibly lending a hand to fate, Waite encouraged Barney to use his great promotion skills and put together a trip for Reds fans to travel to Milwaukee for a critical series with the Braves. Waite and the sponsor, Burger Beer, would advertise the trip during the ballgame broadcast and get the fans excited to root for the Reds.

The rest is history. Barney formed the Red Rooters Club and over six-hundred Reds fans went by train to Milwaukee. The Rapp family even made more than six-hundred sandwiches for box lunches to serve on the train. This was the start of over sixty years of Red Rooters trips that are still going strong today; trips to every National League Park, and many American League Parks, including the World Series in 1990 at Oakland and trips to Cooperstown for Reds inductions into the National Baseball Hall of Fame.

Red Rooters at spring training.

Into the Fire

In 1964, I went on my first Red Rooters trip by train to the West Coast. We left Cincinnati's Union Terminal with eighty Rooters headed to Nevada and California. We would see the Reds play in San Francisco vs. the Giants and then in Los Angeles vs. the Dodgers, with additional stops in Reno and Las Vegas.

At that time I wasn't yet in the tour business, I was taking a working vacation with my wife, Susie, helping out my father-in-law, Barney, with our large contingent of Reds fans. This was my first trip escorting fans and it very well could have been my last.

The first leg of our train journey was from Cincinnati to Chicago. On arrival in the windy city, we met buses that would transfer us to Chicago's Union Station where we would board the Super Chief train to the west. We were really excited. It was my first trip to these destinations.

When we arrived at Union Station, I was confronted by several of our Rooters who informed me that one of the individuals from our group was very intoxicated, using very bad language, and being very disrespectful to some of our guests. I went to find Barney to tell him about the situation. He gave me the man's train ticket, telling me to send him home, and that we would send him a refund. Barney sent me off with a "hurry up" as our train for the west coast would be leaving in five minutes. By this time, everyone else had boarded the train and I was all alone searching for the inebriated man. I finally found him and immediately he asked, "Where did everyone go?" I told him they were all on the train and that the train was leaving, but he wasn't going to be boarding the train with us. I gave him his return ticket to Cincinnati, quickly told him about the refund, bid him goodbye, left him in the station, and ran down to the gate entrance where I boarded the train just before it slowly started to leave the station. Susie was very nervous that I wasn't going to be able to be on the train and was relieved when she saw me board. I relaxed as the problem was now solved, and started to enjoy the ride.

The next day we were walking through the train to the club car and guess who I saw sitting at the bar with a drink in his hand? Frank, the guy I gave the ticket to go back to Cincinnati. How he was able to navigate his way back in the Chicago station, in his condition, find the train, and board it in the time before our immediate departure is a mystery to this day that I can't imagine solving.

The train continued westward and we next encountered a flood in Nebraska which caused us to back up for a while and detour around the Platt River. While doing this I encountered my next challenge. One of our guests came up to me and told me he was paired as a roommate with another man that he didn't know. He went on to disclose that at every stop the train made, his roommate would take his luggage off of the overhead rack and get ready to get off the train. I began to investigate. I found the roommate and was about to inquire as to what might have been wrong; but, before I could ask, he looked me square in the eye and said, *"The Lawrence Welk Show* was great last night." To say the least, I was puzzled. Our itinerary did indeed have a scheduled stop to see Lawrence Welk, but that was going to be in Los Angeles much later in the trip. That was my first clue that this was going to be problem number two. I asked if he felt all right and he told me he had recently hit his head by falling off a ladder, but his nephew insisted he take this trip on his own. Clearly he was not in a good mental state, so I located the train conductor and suggested we get the passenger off the train and send him back home to Cincinnati.

We were now in Ogden, Utah, and the conductor said he would take him to the train master's office at our next stop, Salt Lake City. The conductor asked for his ticket. Unfortunately, all of the tickets for our group were with Barney and he was in a Pullman sleeping car, thirteen cars forward from the coach cars where we were riding.

It was about 1:00 a.m., so many of the train's passengers had already dozed off for the night. They wouldn't stay restful for long though. I held onto the gentlemen with one hand and his piece of luggage in the other, and starting walking forward, car by car, through the aisles, banging the sleeping passengers in the head through twelve rail cars. When we finally reached the Pullman section I tried opening the passage door, but it was locked. After knocking hard for several minutes, a sleepy conductor appeared and asked what I wanted. After explaining the situation, he informed me that his car was a staff car and we would not be allowed to pass through. Instead, we would have to go back to our assigned car until the train arrived in Salt Lake City. Only then could we get off the train and walk up beyond the thirteen cars to the Pullman section to get the ticket from Mr. Rapp. Back through the twelve cars we went, knocking the same people in the head for a second time as we passed down the aisle of each car.

When we stopped in Salt Lake City and got off the train, I was told by the Station Master to hurry as the train would leave in twenty minutes and that I had to hold on to the man until I came back to the station with him and his ticket for home. We walked up the long platform and reached Barney's car, woke him up, got the ticket and were ready to walk back to the station when with a jolt, his car was disconnected from the coach cars and we were slowly moving, in the dead of the night, out into the train yard. By the time the train stopped, we had lost a bit of time and had to quickly step off and make our way over tracks and switches back to the station. The other coach section was being hooked up to an engine and was getting ready to leave. With one hand on my friend and the other holding his luggage, I shouted that we were back and handed off the man, his luggage, and his ticket to the Station Master who had ordered an ambulance to take the man to the hospital for observation.

Exhausted, but relieved, I started to board the train. It was then I was met by another of our guests who greeted me by saying, "This is a beautiful home you have," and "Wasn't the show we saw tonight wonderful?" I could only imagine that I was in a nightmare that wouldn't end. Two men going goofy in one night? His wife was hysterical and kept saying, "I told his doctor he shouldn't be traveling, but the doctor said the trip would be good for him." I yelled to the Station Master, "Hold the ambulance, I got two more for you!" As the wife started down the train steps she slipped and cut her knee. Good thing they were headed to the hospital. I told the Station Master we would wire the ticket numbers when we arrived at our destination the next morning, as the Pullman section with Barney and the tickets had already left. I boarded the train physically and mentally exhausted with three less members of our group left in Salt Lake City.

The next morning, we arrived in Las Vegas and transferred by bus to the Flamingo Hotel which still looked like it did when it was originally built by the mobster Bugsy Siegel. After checking in the group, I heard a page for Mr. Barney Rapp who was wanted on the telephone. He hadn't arrived yet with the others who purchased Pullman class tickets, so I took the phone call. It was his secretary calling from Cincinnati asking what happened to the first passenger I took off the train in the middle of the night. She said the Salt Lake City police had found him wandering alone in the city, without shoes or luggage. The only thing the police found on him was a train ticket inside a Barney Rapp Agency folder that included the agency's phone number. I told her what had occurred the night before and couldn't believe he had gotten away from the railroad official. She promised to contact his nephew and have him arrange for his return home. I finally collapsed into a lobby chair, next to my wife, totally wiped-out from this adventure. Just a moment later, Barney and his small group of well-rested, freshly-showered people strolled into the lobby. Barney found me sleeping in a lobby chair and immediately woke me up with a firm, "I brought you along to help out, not take naps." He had no idea what we had gone through during the night. I looked over at Susie and told her I may have to give the responsibilities back to her dad and go home. Well, I didn't do either. I stuck it out and the rest of the trip was wonderful.

By the way, if you are wondering what happened to Frank, our intoxicated guest; he continued being a problem. In San Francisco we didn't see him for two days and when we finally tracked him down, he was so drunk that we had to put him in the shower, clean him up, sober him up, and make the decision that we would keep him close to us for the rest of the trip. We obviously made a note that we didn't want him to book any future tours with us.

Upon our arrival in Nevada, we stayed at a hotel in Sparks called the Nugget. It featured a show that had Bertha the elephant as an attraction. One of our guests complained that his room had only a double bed and that he and his wife had been sleeping in separate beds for many years. The hotel was completely sold out as Al Hirt, the famous trumpet player, was performing there and guests were not checking out until the next day. They would have to share the double bed for the night. The next morning, the guest and his wife were told that the hotel could now move them into a room with two beds. I was explaining on the phone that the bellman would be coming to get their luggage when the husband said, "Listen, this is the first time we have slept

Cindy Rapp, Barney Rapp, Susie, and Herb at the "Nugget," in Sparks, Nevada, with Bertha the elephant, who was the main attraction.

together in years and we want to keep our room. In fact, please make sure we have the same room arrangements for the rest of the trip." So, with the bad, you take the good.

Barney knew how to make this a great trip, as he did for many years. He had hired bands to play for our sections at both Dodger Stadium and Candlestick Park, where we sat and rooted for our Reds. We went to Disneyland, Farmer's Market, Fisherman's Wharf, and so much more. The train trip back home was, thankfully, uneventful. This was a wonderful first trip with the Red Rooters in spite of a shaky start; and, it was the first of many more.

Play Ball

The second trip that Susie and I took with the Red Rooters was to spring training in Tampa, Florida. This was in the mid-1960s and again, we traveled by train. Our large contingent of over two-hundred Rooters left Cincinnati Union Terminal early on Saturday morning. We had four coach cars, a Pullman car, and a baggage car with a bar loaded with over one hundred cases of Burger Beer, the radio sponsor of the Reds. The car was open twenty-four hours for free beverages. Joe Gramke, a well-known Cincinnati policeman, always took his vacation and worked with Barney on many of the trips. He was in charge of the bar.

We stopped our train in Jacksonville, Florida, as the Southern Railroad terminated there and switched over to Seaboard Railroad. While this transfer of engines took several hours due to schedules, the group was provided with breakfast in the Station Coffee Shop; and, being a Sunday, Barney provided transportation to those who wished to attend worship services in town.

Our arrival in Tampa was a grand affair. As we got off the train and onto our buses, we were part of a large parade through town with a band, cheerleaders, and hosts passing out orange juice and Hava-Tampa cigars. We stayed at the Floridian Hotel and Barney hosted an "Over-the-Rhine" dinner for the Rooters featuring German style food. As a fun contest, Barney drew names awarding winners with a free ten-minute long-distance call back home. That was a big deal back then. There was a huge banquet during the week where the Reds' players and wives attended and the team manager, coaches, and announcers were also there. The banquet program was even broadcast live on the radio back to Cincinnati. In addition to the ballgames, we visited places like Busch Gardens, Parrot Jungle, Cypress Gardens, Derby Lane Greyhound Racing, and had special meals at the Kapok Tree and Causeway Inn Restaurants. Barney would have a four-piece pep band at each game and he would play the bass drum. This became a highlight each spring. Spring training was an exciting week, unlike anything else at that time for professional sports fans. We never could have imagined how amazing these trips would be in the next decades.

Extra Innings

Barney kept growing the Red Rooters' Club and added other destinations to the already successful West Coast and Spring Training trips. We traveled to the other baseball cities in our region, via motor coach trips to St. Louis, Chicago, Pittsburgh, Atlanta, and combination trips to New Orleans/Houston. Beyond baseball, he also did a trip to the New York World's Fair and added an annual December tour to the Orange Bowl in Miami including the parade, a New Year's Eve party and a three- or four-day cruise. It seemed that no location was out of reach.

The Houston Astrodome was billed as the Eighth Wonder of the World, by Judge Roy Hoffheinz, therefore it was an obvious addition to our slate. The enormous, domed stadium opened in 1965. Barney advertised a trip to the Astrodome that included the University of Cincinnati/University of Houston football game one evening, followed by a conversion of the stadium for the start of the Cincinnati Reds vs. the Houston Astros series the very next day. There were three chartered aircrafts taking a huge Cincinnati crowd to see two hometown teams play in this amazing facility. The night of the football game, among the Cincinnati fans, I sat with Barney and his friend Waite Hoyt. It was September, close to the end of the season and Waite was going to retire, making this his last road trip broadcasting. He asked if I would like to sit with him the next two nights in the broadcast booth and hand him the scores of other games coming off of the ticker tape. Claude Sullivan, his partner, was not with him as he was broadcasting University of Kentucky football games. I couldn't believe this was happening to me. I didn't hesitate to say, "Yes," and for the next two nights I sat with Waite. After the game, it was my job to get a taxi and bring him to our hotel where we had an after-game party. Wow, what a job! Waite became a great friend. More about him later.

Barney Rapp passed away suddenly at the age of seventy, shortly after the 1970 World Series. He was a tremendous promoter and entertainer, and beloved by so many. His wife, Ruby Wright Rapp, took over the agency and my long-time friend and colleague, Jim Mogan, helped her run the baseball trips during the summer break from his school year position as a principal in the Dayton school system. In October of 1974, I joined the Barney Rapp Agency as a full-time employee and in 1976, we became Barney Rapp Travel, a full-line travel agency. Shortly afterwards as business grew and many more trips became part of the itinerary, Jim Mogan also came aboard full-time.

The Machine Years

The 1970s were the years of the Big Red Machine. Winning Division titles and pennants, and playing in and winning the World Series became pretty common and expected events. Everyday players like Pete Rose, Johnny Bench, Tony Perez, George Foster, Ken Griffey Sr., Cesar Geronimo, Dave Conception, and pitchers like Jack Billingham, Don Gullet, and others were what made the machine run on all cylinders.

Our Red Rooter trips were running full. The spring training trip to Tampa, Florida, averaged seven hundred fans per year. We now split the travel between chartered airplanes and motor coaches. Our group filled three hotels and required enormous ballrooms to seat us for our dinner events. We packed specialty restaurants like the Kapok Tree and The Festhaus in Busch Gardens. We had lines of buses take us to the ballpark, Disney World, Cypress Gardens, and other Florida attractions.

A special treat we always included on the trip was our celebrated Baseball Banquet. Bob Braun of WLW Television was our master of ceremonies and all the Reds players, managers, coaches, etc. would attend with their families. We also had special guests like Waite Hoyt, Johnny Vander Meer, and Sparky Anderson speak to our group. It was always a heck of a party. After dinner there was dancing to the music of Jack Golly's big band, plus the additional player from our group, Randy Cobb, who had an array of musical instruments that he brought along with him each year. And there was plenty of free beer and snacks being served up to keep the evening going strong.

Jack Golly, who had played with the Spike Jones orchestra, always had hijinks planned for Randy. One year, Jack had Randy, who was wrapped in a sheet and wearing a turban headdress, sit on a large chair on the stage. Jack had put some kind of powder charge under the seat. The orchestra started to play and boom! The powder ignited and caused so much smoke in the Hyatt Ball-

Barney Rapp playing the drums with the Red Rooters at a spring training game.

room that it set off the smoke alarms causing the fire department to respond. Jack would come up with a new thing to do to Randy each year and Randy was always a good sport.

Those spring training trips were full of both affectionate and electrifying memories for so many people. It's astonishing that during the seventies we would fill as many as seventeen motor coaches with hundreds of Rooters. The logistics of transportation, hotels, and meals for these enormous groups were huge undertakings; but the thrill of the fans watching the Big Red Machine, made it all worth it. Years later, the induction of Johnny Bench, Sparky Anderson, Tony Perez, and Marty Brennaman into the National Baseball Hall of Fame once again brought hundreds of those fans together, this time in Cooperstown.

Spring training for the Cincinnati Reds later moved to Plant City and Sarasota, and now is in Goodyear, Arizona. Sixty years later, the Reds Rooters trips continue each spring, along with motor coach trips throughout the season to watch the Cincinnati Reds play in St. Louis, Pittsburgh, Chicago, Milwaukee, Atlanta, Philadelphia, New York, Detroit, and Cleveland.

Another organization supporting the Cincinnati Reds, was started several years after the formation of the Red Rooters' Club. Barney Rapp helped organize the Rosie Reds which now thrives as a philanthropic and social organization. Over their many years, they have awarded baseball endowments and scholarships to baseball players attending area universities and to Withrow High School. And, each year the Rosies do a trip via motor coach to a ballpark where the Reds are playing.

Over There

In 1976, we decided to take the Red Rooters on a European trip. We chartered a boat for a cruise on the Rhine River with a three-day extension in Switzerland. We had a group of one hundred-fifty, and boy was I nervous handling this large group for my first tour to Europe. We started in Amsterdam and one of the ladies in the group was complaining that her back hurt and I needed to get her Doan's Little Liver Pills. Well, they don't actually sell medicine like that over the counter in Europe, so what were we to do? She continued to complain so my brother-in-law, Ray Nulsen, and another guest and I took her by taxi to a nearby hospital for examination. After waiting quite some time, the doctor escorted her and said we needed to take her to see a private doctor. It was already quite late in the evening. We pulled up to this regular looking private home which was dark. Ringing the bell, the lights came on and we were directed inside. The three of us were instructed to wait in the front room while he took the patient to the rear of the house. As we waited, we curiously looked around the room and noticed all the pictures on the wall and magazines on the tables had images of dogs, cats, horses, and other animals. All the clues led to the conclusion that this doctor must have been a veterinarian! He handed us a prescription and sent us on our way. At the stroke of midnight we finally found a pharmacy that could fill the script. We never were certain about that doctor or the prescription, as the woman never stopped complaining the rest of the trip.

Our first night overseas, we stayed at the Hotel Krasnapolski located on the famous Dam Square near the canals in Amsterdam's Red Light District. It was our arrival day and after an elegant welcome dinner many of us decided to walk along the canal. Upon returning to the hotel I was met by the night manager of the hotel who informed me that one of our guests was upset as her wallet was missing. There she was in the lobby, dressed in her nightgown, hair in rollers, crying, "I try to be so good." I settled her down some and we went to her room to look for the missing wallet. No luck! We looked in the hotel ballroom where we had dinner, also no luck. Back in her room I asked to see inside her suitcase which was locked and, of course, the key was in the wallet. I forced the locks open and still, no wallet. It got very late and our search was far from successful. We were all exhausted so I told her to go to sleep and in the morning I would lend her money for the rest of the trip. Drained, we went to our rooms and called it a night. She was a single passenger with her own room, but her friend was also a single with a room next door. About fifteen minutes later my phone rang and it was her friend calling to tell me she had put the lady to bed and when she puffed the pillows, she found the missing wallet inside the pillow case. Mystery solved but on each of our stops during the rest of the trip, I had to tie her suitcase with a rope as the lock was broken.

While sailing on the Rhine River, we were passing by the famous Lorelei Rock. Two of our passengers were sisters. As one of the sisters was climbing up the outside staircase to the top deck, she missed a step and slid backwards out of sight. It appeared, from our vantage point, that she fell overboard. The other sister saw this and gave out a blood-curdling scream. I can still hear that deafening shriek over forty years later. Several of us ran to the rail ready to throw a life buoy into the river and yell, "Man overboard" when we realized that she had only slipped back a couple of steps and was still with us, only suffering a couple of scrapes on her knees.

On our final evening of this trip, we had an elegant reception and dinner at our hotel, the Grand National in Lucerne. As guests of the hotel director, my mother-in-law Ruby, my sister-in-law Patty, her husband Ray, and I were seated in a stunning spot in the room. Suddenly, a lady from our group came rushing over to our table. She was visibly upset and told us that one of our guests was sick at their table. We ran over as quickly as we could and the guest's wife gave us the particulars on her husband. He had a stomach ache. We started to assist him in standing up so we could take him to the restroom. However, we hadn't realized that this gentleman had unbuckled his belt and loosened his trousers to relieve his pain. As we held him by his arms and started to stand him up, his trousers dropped to his ankles. To watch the expression on the hotel director's face as we struggled to shuffle him along, holding up his pants from the rear, leaving the elegant five-star hotel dining room was priceless. I wish I had a photo.

This was the beginning of many wonderful worldwide trips.

Celebrities

During more than forty-three years organizing excursions, I was fortunate to be part of many trips that were hosted by famous celebrities. It started as a natural fit to have Susie's mom, Ruby Wright Rapp, the president of Barney Rapp Travel, entertain our travelers with her delightful vocals, often accompanied by Cliff Lash. But, it was also a perfect next step to expand our talent roster by inviting other WLW-T personalities from both the Ruth Lyons and Bob Braun shows as our special guest hosts. We started doing Ohio and Mississippi River cruises on the *Delta Queen, Mississippi Queen,* and *American Queen* paddlewheel steamboats. Traveling along with us were Cliff, Marian Spelman, and Bonnie Lou. They would all put on a private show for our group in the Paddlewheel Lounge. It was an extremely unique experience and our guests loved both performances and the opportunity to be with the individuals they got to know from watching television.

Of all the Cincinnati television personalities we traveled with, none seemed more popular than the many trips we took with Bob and Wray Jean Braun. Our first venture, starting in 1980, was Bob's annual trip to Hawaii. That first year we took four-hundred-

Bonnie Lou, Milt Okun, Ruby Wright Rapp, Cliff Lash, and Marian Spelman aboard the *Mississippi Queen* in 1986.

thirty-six guests to four Hawaiian Islands. Bob brought along his wife, Wray Jean, and their three children, Rob, Doug, and Melissa. This annual trip brought back more and more repeaters each year.

Bob was magic. He would go on TV the first week of January to advertise the trip and it would sell out in less than two weeks. Bob was a phenomenal entertainer and his fans loved him so. After his show in Cincinnati went off the air, he moved to Los Angeles where he did television and movie work. Several years later, on returning to Cincinnati, he had his own radio show. The Barney Rapp Travel agency was one of his sponsors and we started doing a variety of trips from Missouri to Europe. On our first of many successful trips to Branson, Bob sold eleven bus loads and we took over five hundred people.

On a trip to New York City one February, we landed in a snow storm. That evening we attended a special event starring Rosemary Clooney in the Rainbow and Stars Room on the 62nd floor of the NBC Building. Rosemary asked Bob to introduce her as we had brought eighty of the one-hundred guests that filled the room. It was snowing so hard even the splendid lights of the New York sky-scrapers couldn't be seen out the windows. Everywhere you looked outside was white. Bob gave a lovely introduction to Rosemary who came out singing, "The Weather Outside is Frightful." What an extraordinary evening! Bob and I were very close friends. It was so difficult to see him ill, later in his life, as he was such a healthy specimen and he left us much too soon. I miss him very much. My wife, Susie, and Wray Jean remained dear friends for many years.

Ruby Wright Rapp.

Swiss Miss

Another of Bob Braun's trips, this one to Europe, started in Switzerland, my favorite country to visit. As a prelude to a Rhine River Cruise, we had a large group of over 110 and staying at the five-star Lucerne Palace Hotel, located right on the lake.

One of our couples on the trip lived in a retirement community. The husband was a very large man and his wife was very small, about five-feet tall. One day we were standing in the hotel lobby when the husband came down to the lobby area excitedly shouting, "Where is that woman?" He went on to inform us that he couldn't find his wife and somehow, she had gone missing. We told him to calm down and let our staff search for her, confident we would quickly find her. Unfortunately after searching high and low for an hour, we still hadn't had any luck and he was getting very upset. Cautiously, we had even looked in the lake, just in case. The man's emotions seemed to be taking a toll on him, so we encouraged him to return to his room to lie down while we continued the search. He finally relented and we took him up to his room to rest. He took off his shoes and plopped onto the bed when abruptly a loud scream came out of the covers. Yes, his wife had been in bed the entire time. Being so short, she had slid down in the bed, down deep in the covers, and was fast asleep out of sight. All of our fears that she had fallen in the lake were eased. Whew!

Later that afternoon, the same couple came down to the elegant lobby area and were standing in front of the concierge desk looking at travel folders.

What I'm about to tell you is the absolute truth about a very unfortunate situation, but I must relate this to you. Apparently the wife had eaten something that didn't quite agree with her because all of a sudden and very unexpectedly, we heard a very loud flatulence (gas) accompanied by an uncontrolled deposit on the floor in front of the concierge desk. The hotel's concierge, dressed

Bob Braun Group, Switzerland-Rhine Cruise, 1982. I am in the very front on the left.

in his tails and white starched collar, both heard and saw the outcome. Aghast, he peered over his gold rimmed glasses at the floor and uttered loudly in German, "WAS IST DAS?" (What is that?)

After hearing the reverberating back-blast bomb and the aftermath of what was on the floor, we took off for the front door. The last thing we heard as we ran out of the hotel was the husband yelling, "Damn it woman!" Since that trip, I have stayed at that hotel many times and often stare at the area where this happened. I half expect to see a star in the floor, like on the Hollywood Walk of Fame. Fortunately, I have never seen the concierge who was on duty that fateful day, again.

Funny Incidents

When you do trips together, like Bob Braun and I did, there are bound to be numerous laughable tales shared along the way.

On one of our ocean cruises we had a lady passenger who used one of the ship's restrooms. She locked the outer door, inner door, and the one in the stall. She had been in there for quite a while when her husband started yelling for her through the outer door. She shouted back that she was stuck in the stall and the door wouldn't open. Due to the fact that the outer and inner doors were also locked from the inside, no one could get inside to help her. Finally, we had to call on the ship's engineer who had to saw through both doors to reach the woman in the stall. By the time she was reached, a large crowd had gathered outside the restroom to watch the daring rescue. It was much more exciting than playing Jackpot Bingo.

As a result of having large crowds travel with us, I would often bring along assistants to help. One of the most colorful was Larry Wettenkamp, a former school teacher and a part-time maître d' at various restaurants. Larry was a good man to have around. First of all, on two separate occasions he was in the right place and gave the Heimlich maneuver to two separate individuals who were choking on their food, essentially saving their lives. Secondly, Larry was easy to get along with and happy to be in on the fun, even at his own expense.

On a flight to Hawaii, our American Airlines representative upgraded Larry to a seat in first class. Larry had never sat in that class of service before. When the flight attendant offered Larry a menu for lunch, he looked it over and not seeing any prices, he tried to calculate in his head what the cost would be for what he wanted to order. He figured a steak would be about $30 with a salad, dessert, coffee, and a drink adding another $30 to the bill. With the addition of an in-flight movie, estimated cost $10, Larry guessed his total bill would be $70. He approached me quietly and said he didn't have enough cash on him to pay for all he had ordered. I happily told him, restraining my laughter, that I would take care of it and he could pay me later. He obviously didn't know that all of this was free in first class.

On the way back home he was again seated in first class. I told our American Airlines representative to get a piece of airline stationery and when we arrived back at our airport he was to hand Larry an official looking invoice. On the invoice the tally for his flight included Meals/$110, Movies/$20, Drinks/$50, Pillow/$10, Blanket/$10, Life Vest/$15, Flight Attendant Gratuity/$25, Oxygen Masks/$15, Upgrade to First Class/$200 with the total amount due upon landing $455.00. Upon looking at the invoice, Larry was in shock, red in the face, and looking frantic. Finally, we all burst out laughing and said, "Welcome to First Class, Larry!" Needless to say, he was relieved, but he was also a very good sport.

Rosemary

Nick and Nina Clooney have not only been dear friends but very popular hosts on many of our trips to Lake Tahoe, Hawaii, and Europe. Among the many travels, there was one trip that became a trip of a lifetime for a wonderful group of forty-six of our travelers. Upon my request, Nick asked his sister Rosemary if she would be interested in joining us on a trip. Much to our delight, she accepted. So, in 1989, Nick and Nina, along with Rosemary and her future husband Dante DiPaolo, embarked on an amazing trip to England. Dante was a well-known dancer/actor with film credits from *Seven Brides for Seven Brothers* to *Sweet Charity*.

Our group left Cincinnati for New York City and began our journey with lunch at the famous Tavern on the Green. We then transferred to the Hudson River Pier to board the magnificent *QEII* for a five day transatlantic cruise to England. To the delight of the ship's passengers, during the ocean crossing, Rosemary Clooney put on two fabulous performances accompanied by the ship's orchestra. At each of the performances, she revealed that she was with a group from Cincinnati. She went on to mention that I had not only arranged this trip for our group, but that I was the son-in-law of Barney Rapp, the band leader and agent that started both Rosemary and her sister Betty on their professional singing careers.

It was beyond thrilling to sit at dinner each evening with Nick, Nina, Rosemary, and Dante and listen to the many stories they recounted.

Rosemary recollected her purchase of George Gershwin's home in Beverly Hills. One day, George's brother, Ira, who happened to live next door, stopped over to visit Rosemary and noticed that her piano was located in the same spot where his brother George would compose on his piano. Ira told her that at one instance he came into the house and George was composing a song about a dreary day in London. He was struggling to come

Herb, Rosemary Clooney, Nick Clooney, Nina Clooney, and Dante DiPaolo on the *Queen Elizabeth II* in 1989.

Inside the Concorde, 1989. Herb is in the second row on the far right.

up with a title. Sitting together at the piano the brother duo finally came up with one—"A Foggy Day in London Town."

Rosemary also told us of the wonderful Christmas parties
she hosted at her home. Her dear friend, Bing Crosby, would sit
facing the fireplace, pipe in his mouth. Inevitably, he would be
asked to sing, "I'm Dreaming of a White Christmas," and without taking his pipe out of his mouth, he would break into his
rendition of the Irving Berlin's seasonal anthem.

Our trip on the *QEII* ended with our arrival in Southampton
where we checked into the luxurious London Ritz Hotel for a
few nights. While in London we did all the usual touring, saw
a show at the London Palladium, and even took a trip on the

Orient Express train from Folkston back to London, having high tea with scones, clotted cream, and jam. The cherry on top of the trip was our flight home. Our group flew back to New York on the Concorde in about three hours. Seeing the earth's curvature, 60,000 feet above the world below, was beyond astonishing.

What an unforgettable trip and all the Clooney's were delightful hosts. We later did another trip with all four of them on the *Mississippi Queen*, sailing from New Orleans. Rosemary once again performed for the passengers and everyone enjoyed being with these down-home Kentucky folks.

Ship Tales

The talent-hosted trips didn't always go without a hitch though. On a WLW radio advertisers' trip to French Polynesia, Bill Cunningham, The Great American, was one of the hosts. During a cocktail reception aboard ship, he got up to make a speech on behalf of the station. He wanted to start the trip out with a bang, so he immediately stated that he had met Jesus. He was, of course, referring to his dining room waiter, Jesus. The mood wasn't quite so jovial the next day however. While anchored off the island of Bora Bora, I was summoned by Bill's wife to come down to their cabin as Bill was very sick.

On entering the cabin I saw Bill in bed, shivering, wrapped in a sheet. He exclaimed he was in serious pain and the ship's doctor, who only spoke French, told him it could be a kidney stone or maybe something worse. I asked him if the pain was in his back, moving forward towards his stomach and if he was having trouble going to the bathroom. Answering in the affirmative to all of my questions I told him my guess was that he was having a kidney stone problem. He asked me how I knew and I told him I had endured five of those and his symptoms seemed spot on. Without hesitation, he declared he wanted to go home!

Usually, a few calls and this task could be accomplished fairly quickly, but we were anchored off of Bora Bora. It was going to be a little more difficult to get him off the ship and arrange for him to get home. I suggested he drink lots of water with the hope that he could pass the stone. Insisting that he wanted to leave, my associate, Joel Pieper, started making inquiries to complete the arrangements. Air Tahiti Nui informed us that the only way to get him home was to secure a small launch to take them from our ship over to Bora Bora; charter a flight to fly them from Bora Bora to Papeete; reserve a hotel so they could stay overnight in Papeete; fly the next day to Los Angeles; and, finally fly back to Cincinnati. I asked if he was sure they wanted to do all of that and he answered with a resounding, "Yes." We quickly helped get them packed and ready for the transfers, as we were getting close to our departure. Reluctantly, but knowing too well the pain he was in, I passed him a small bottle of pain medicine from a recent post-surgery prescription of mine, "just in case."

Bill and his wife appeared at the ships landing platform. Clearly, Bill was in a great amount of discomfort. The small launch arrived and we waved goodbye as they started to sail away. A few minutes later the ship's purser came running with their passports in her hand as they forgot to give them to them as they left. Of course, the launch was out of sight. The ship had to radio the launch and tell them to return, as they would not be able to continue their journey home without their passports. About fifteen minutes later, they reappeared; Bill looking much worse than before. The passports were handed off and they departed for a second time. We faintly heard Bill's anguished tone asking his wife for a pill, and they sailed away once more. That was the last we saw or heard from them for a few days until we called and found that Bill had gone to the hospital at home, passed the stone and was now feeling fine.

Once our group had returned from our amazing voyage, Bill was back on the air at WLW and we all got to hear the rest of the story. His show started with the subject of his adventure in French Polynesia. He first named me Citizen-of-the-Year, for saving his life and then he went on to tell the story of what happened to him and his wife after leaving our ship.

Their trip home started with the landing of the water launch on Bora Bora where they were transported to a small airstrip and left there, alone. Sitting there with their luggage, waiting for the plane to take them to Papeete, there was not a single soul in sight. Waiting and waiting, Bill started to question if anyone was coming to pick them up. "We're stranded and we are going to die here," Bill uttered to his wife, Penny. Finally, they heard the drone of a plane in the distance. "I hear the plane! I see the plane," Bill continued. And, with that, a small plane landed and off to Papeete they went. However, it was not a smooth flight. A storm developed with rain, thunder, and lightning and once again, the impending doom set in. Bill whispered to Penny, "We are going to die and I have pain, give me another pill." They finally saw the lights of Papeete and landed. Still complaining of the pain, Bill asked for yet another pill and Penny, worried, asked him, "Do you want to go to a hospital?" Bill retorted, "No, just give me another pill." He stuck it out for the night and the next morning boarded the plane back to Los Angeles and then Cincinnati.

On the broadcast with the background musical accompaniment of the "Elephant Walk" theme, Bill said, "Don't ever go to French Polynesia." After his show I called Bill at home. "You set back tourism to French Polynesia probably by ten years," I joked with him and reminded him of the picture I took of him at a beach party, the day before he got sick, with one hand holding a tropical drink in a coconut shell and the other arm around two beautiful Polynesian native girls posing with him. In addition, I told him he got me in trouble with the DEA who interrogated me for giving Type 2 narcotics to him. I had him going for a while until we both broke out laughing. This story is now a classic Cunningham tale, and has been played on the radio several times. I even have a copy if you are in need of a laugh.

On another WLW trip to the Mediterranean, we were anchored off the coast of Monaco. It was the trial week of the Grand Prix and we had to take the tender boats from the ship to the shore, and back again. The last tender from the pier back to the ship was at 11:00 p.m. which has always been plenty of time for the ship's passengers that were out and about in town. But, not this time! Two of our gentlemen guests missed the last tender back to the ship. Somehow they came up with what must have seemed an ingenious plan at the time. The tender boat might have left the pier, but the area was filled with fancy yachts from all over the world, visiting Monaco for the week's upcoming events. Since they couldn't make it back aboard ship for the night and they needed somewhere to sleep, they hopped onto a couple of the empty yachts and those became their dwellings for the evening.

The next morning they left their extravagant sleeping quarters and somehow managed to get back to our ship. That evening, our last before disembarking in Nice, France, we had a farewell cocktail reception on the open deck. The station sales manager asked me to rouse the two individuals with a made-up story of how much trouble they were now in. Always up for a little good fun and trickery, I accepted the challenge. They were in a jovial mood, enjoying the cocktail party, when I approached. With an extremely serious tone, I told them that when we arrived in Nice the next morning, Interpol would be waiting to speak to them. I went on to report that, unfortunately, one of them had ended up sleeping on the Swiss ambassador's yacht and the other on the Turkish ambassador's yacht and in both instances valuable jewelry was missing; and, they were both persons of interest.

Their fun-loving demeanor immediately changed. With faces that first presented an embarrassing red tone, instantaneously followed by ghostly-white fear, they protested that they didn't do it! I suggested they might want to secure an attorney; and, luckily with Bill Cunningham on board, perhaps he could defend them. I also informed them that proactively I had changed their airline tickets to return home from Nice a week later than previously scheduled, as the police were known as being very slow at interrogating suspects. I believe they both were about to faint or have an accident when the sales manager, who had been standing behind them listening all along, burst out laughing. They turned around upon hearing the laughs and realized they were caught in a hoax. Both of them looked at the manager and in unison exclaimed, "You son of a bitch." The manager proceeded to give me a "high five" and nodded with, "You get the Academy Award for the Best Performance."

We never know what might be waiting around the corner on some of these voyages, but we usually get at least a fun tale to tell once we arrive home.

Lost and Found

As anyone who travels frequently can tell you, on occasion, things go missing. Luggage is delayed, electronics are left at TSA, and items are forgotten at home. Along many travels, I have witnessed my share of occasions when items became lost; but also, luckily, later found.

On one of the Bob Braun Hawaii trips, as a nice fatherly gesture, Bob had given each of his three children a $100 bill to use as spending money. No sooner had the money been given then it was gone. I had just made my way to the hotel's beach when I ran into Rob Braun, Bob's son and the news anchor on Cincinnati's WKRC-TV for many years. Rob said he had put his $100 bill in his swimsuit pocket and headed out into the ocean. When he came back to shore, the money had vanished. He searched the area where he had been swimming, but the waves had surely taken it away. About a half hour later, one of the hotel's water sports attendants emerged from the ocean, excited that he had found a $100 bill floating in the water! I approached him and I told him I knew to whom it belonged. Of course, he did not want to believe me—who would? But, I went on to insist that the $100 bill belonged to Mr.

Braun's son and that they had brought over four-hundred people to stay at the hotel. Wouldn't it be a great gesture if he offered it back? He finally agreed to return the money and received a nice reward. One never knows what treasures the ocean holds.

On another occasion, during a trip to Switzerland, our group went on a tour of Lucerne with our longtime friend and guide Heidi Mahrer. Generously, she invited the group back to her house for a drink and dessert after the tour. Heidi has a beautiful home on Lake Lucerne with a magnificent view of nearby Mt. Rigi, so it was certainly a wonderful bonus for the group. My wife, Susie, and I didn't take the tour, but planned to join the group at Heidi's house.

Bob Braun and Herb in Hawaii.

We left our hotel in a taxi to head to Heidi's. It was a bright, sunny day, so once settled inside the taxi, I decided to switch my regular prescription glasses for my prescription sunglasses. I laid my regular glasses on the seat beside me and just enjoyed the view outside. On arriving at Heidi's house I reached for my regular glasses, to make the switch back, and realized I didn't have them. I had left them in the taxi. I tried to call the taxi company, but no one answered. Oh no. I started to worry. Would I have to wear my sunglasses for the remainder of the trip? When we got back to our hotel, I tried calling the taxi company again; still no answer. I struggled to recall everything I could and all I could remember was that the taxi was painted red and their telephone number was II-II-II-IIII. To make matters worse, the hotel concierge said that particular taxi company didn't ring any bells with him.

Remaining hopeful, later in the afternoon as Susie and I were walking down Lucerne's main street, I suggested we stop on the corner for a minute and just see if any taxis would drive by. I figured we could flag them down and try to find a way to call the taxi where I left my glasses. Suddenly, off in the distance, we spotted a red taxi coming our way. We immediately started waving furiously and the taxi pulled over. Amazingly, it was the same woman driving the taxi! She opened her window and in her outstretched hand were my glasses. What are the odds that we would be standing on that very spot, at that very hour, and that very same taxi would drive by, returning my glasses only hours after I lost them. I wished they had Powerball lotteries back then. I would have played!

We've actually had luck on our side a few times, like the time we were in Germany. Susie always had a favorite red card case that held her credit cards, driver's license, and a little bit of emergency cash. We had just finished our group tour to Heidelberg, had lunch, and returned to the ship. After taking a short nap, Susie was looking for the red case and couldn't find it. We emptied all our bags, tore the bed apart, searched our cabin, and called the restaurant where we had lunch. No luck. We called American Express to cancel her card and they informed us that they had a service that would cancel her other credit cards and her driver's license; and, have new cards and license issued and waiting for when we returned home. We accepted their help and thought, "What a great service!"

The next morning, we were waiting for the motor coach to come to our ship for another local tour. Our group was a Joe Nuxhall sponsored trip, as he had retired from broadcasting Reds games and wanted to go on a Rhine River cruise through Germany. As the motor coach approached, I immediately recognized it as the same coach we were on the day before. It still had the Joe Nuxhall Group sign in the window. I jumped on board and looked under the seat where Susie and I were sitting, hoping to find the card case, but didn't see it. I looked a little closer and there, stuck in the gap between the two seats, I glimpsed the top corner of the missing case. I jumped off the coach and ran to Susie to give her the good news. Another miracle, the missing red case was found. Even better news, she couldn't buy anything with her credit cards for the rest of the trip because they had all been canceled. One more miracle!

Reggie Williams, Steve Cauthen, Herb, Marty Brennaman, and Joe Nuxhall.

Two of our frequent passengers and good friends, Rusty and Renee Frankel, have also provided us with several challenging situations. On one of our All-Star Cruises, they went to Ft. Lauderdale a day prior to the cruise departure and stayed at a local motel that had a kitchen with a table top range. On preparing to repack and join the ship, Rusty placed his suitcase on the counter top where the stove top was located. Somehow the control knob was twisted and the range was turned on. His suitcase caught on fire, sending smoke into the room, setting off the alarms, and bringing the fire department to the room.

Cleverly, Rusty called his son back home to pack another suitcase, including a suit he needed, and bring it to my house so

I could take it to the ship when we left the next day. I delivered the suitcase on board our ship but it turned out that the suit his son sent was the wrong size; so, he had to rent a tuxedo for the formal nights.

On another occasion, Renee Frankel forgot her passport and couldn't get on the ship without the passport or a certified copy of her birth certificate. Fortunately, she was able to contact the board of health back home and they faxed a certified copy of her birth certificate; so, she was able to sail. The Frankels are a great couple. Renee practiced law for many years and Rusty is a retired periodontist and a wonderful photographer who creates our group pictures from many of our tours.

Personal items aren't the only things we've seen lost or left behind. On a Red Rooter trip to Atlanta in the mid 1970s we were staying at a hotel on Peachtree Street. The room we had was one of four very special rooms in the hotel. What made it quite different was that each of these rooms had its own pool. I was with my family including Susie, our daughter Julie, son Steve and my mother Sarah. As an added family bonus, we brought my nephew Brad Reisenfeld, who was slightly older than my kids. On one of weekend days at the hotel, we entrusted Brad to take our son Steve, who was then about five years old, down to the lobby. They got on the elevator, arrived at the lobby and somehow Brad got off, but Steve was still on the elevator when the doors closed.

Now this poor little boy was on his own, riding the elevator up and down when anyone called for the elevator on their floor. We were panicked and raced up to various floors hoping and praying that the elevator door would open and there would be Steve. Finally after what seemed like forever, the door on the 5th floor opened. There he was calm, cool, and collected, having a great time. What a relief! Needless to say we didn't trust Brad to look after him anymore on that trip. Even though Brad is now a very accomplished attorney with five kids and several grandchildren of his own, we still tease him about the infamous elevator ride where he lost Steve; and, we will never let him forget it.

Unfortunately, on occasion, we've had things lost to never return. On our first trip to Japan in 1978 to see the Reds play exhibition games, we flew via Anchorage, Alaska. We stopped overnight at the Captain Cook Hotel, did a city sightseeing and were scheduled to continue our flight on Northwest Airlines the next morning to Tokyo. This is what they called the Polar Route to Asia.

Our group was to put all luggage outside our room doors that morning for pickup by the bellman. I was down in the lobby checking off luggage as it arrived to insure every piece was brought down before we left the hotel. I noticed that one of the pieces belonging to my mother-in-law Ruby hadn't arrived. When she came down I asked her if she had put it outside her door. She responded that she had placed two pieces outside, one of which was there, but one that seemed to have gone missing. We searched the floors, hallways, everywhere, but the piece of luggage was not to be found. Obviously it had been stolen.

We left Anchorage without her main piece of luggage that contained most of her clothing including undergarments. When we arrived in Tokyo, we went to a department store so she could purchase what she needed. The language barrier was unbelievable. She couldn't make the salesgirl understand what she wanted to buy. They went into a dressing room and Ruby had to show the salesgirl items she was wearing to make it obvious as to what she needed. She was able to get a few things for the trip, but the cost of the articles of clothing was astronomical compared to the same in the U.S.

We learned a lesson after that not to put luggage outside your door. You never know who might be going around wearing your underwear!

White Suit

That Red Rooters trip to Asia was memorable for many other reasons. Besides getting to witness the Cincinnati Reds play in Japan, we visited several different stadiums and got to see Sadaharu Oh, the Japanese home run king. The trip included stops in Hong Kong, Manila, Japan, and Singapore.

Our group's first stop was Hong Kong for a few days. One of our forty passengers on the trip was a little person who I will call "Bill." Two very memorable incidents involving Bill happened during the trip. Being in Hong Kong, many of our group members, both ladies and men, visited our Hong Kong tailor, Mr. Lee. We ordered suits, shirts, shoes etc. all tailor-made in a couple of days after several selections and fittings. Bill wanted an all-white suit and special shoes. The night prior to our leaving Hong Kong many of us returned to the tailor shop to try on and pay for our final merchandise. On returning to my hotel I got a call from Mr. Lee telling me that Bill had not picked up or paid for his all-white suit. Mr. Lee anxiously inquired, "What I do with little white suit?" I just blurted out the first thing that came to my mind, "Do you know anyone who is having their First Communion?" This of course was a joke and I told him I would get Bill over to him right away to get the white suit, which I did. Bill wore that suit and his custom made shoes for many years.

The other incident with Bill was when we checked into our first hotel in Tokyo. The hotel had assigned Bill a room on the 65th floor of the high rise tower. He called me and said I needed to change his room because he couldn't reach his floor button in the elevator. The button was too high up on the wall. I changed his room to a lower floor and called ahead to the rest of our hotels to make certain to put him on a low floor going forward. You don't usually think about those things that don't affect you, but I never forgot again.

This trip was the last time Pete Rose appeared as a Red as he was traded to Philadelphia the next season. The fans were great and loved the games. Dick Wagner invited our group to a special reception for the team and gave each of us a pin that had both the American and Japanese flag on it with the Reds emblem. It's a wonderful souvenir that I still cherish.

Get Out the Brooms

The Reds won the pennant in 1990 after going wire-to-wire in first place. Now after winning the first two games of the World Series in Cincinnati, we were off to Oakland for games three, four, and five, if necessary. We arrived at the Oakland Athletics ballpark with our group of eighty-four Cincinnati Reds fans. As we stepped off our motor coaches and onto the parking lot, we were greeted by very hostile, threatening fans who were tailgating and consuming some pretty potent beverages. We made our way into the stadium and found our seats. I contacted security to keep an eye on our section just in case we needed protection. In addition to our group, Reds officials, player wives, and owners were also sitting in our section. Things became very quiet as we won game three. With one more win, we would not only be World Champions, but we would have swept the mighty Oakland team.

Now it was game four of the World Series. There was a difference in the crowd, as the possibility of their team being swept hung in the air. They were in a much more subdued mood. Should Oakland win, we had tickets for game five which would be played on Sunday. In case of that fifth game, our travel itinerary had us returning to Cincinnati on Monday. I asked the group for a consensus. If we won the Series on Saturday, would they be interested in going out to a celebration dinner on Sunday at a restaurant I had often frequented in San Francisco. I could return the unused game five tickets and pay for the dinner, plus a tour. Everyone agreed. I called my friend Modesto Lanzone who had a wonderful Italian restaurant and explained the possible last minute situation for Sunday night. He informed me that his restaurant was closed on Sunday. I replied that it was too bad, because I had a nice group. He asked how big a group and when I told him there were eighty-four of us he quickly changed his tune. "What time do you want to be here?" I told him I would call him after the game on Saturday and let him know. Of course, history was made and the Reds swept the A's to become the 1990 World Champions. It was a great dinner celebration and a very memorable trip.

During that fourth game, with the expectancy of the sweep for Cincinnati, *Baseball Today* and the *World Series Highlights* photographers came up to our section to show all the Reds fans live on television. We were also part of the highlight film for the 1990 World Series. Needless to say, the Oakland fans were very quiet except for the many fans that courteously offered congratulations as we left.

Waite-ing for the Rain

Waite Hoyt was a Hall of Fame pitcher for the New York Yankees which in the 1920s was a powerhouse, winning Pennants and World Series. His teammates included Babe Ruth, Lou Gehrig, and the other members of Murderers' Row. Waite was also, after his pitching career, the voice of the Reds. It was during long rain delays that he became noted for his vast amount of baseball stories and the very funny anecdotes of his fellow players. He had a great laugh when telling a story. Waite would sit in the radio station studio during Reds road games and recreate the game pitch-by-pitch, inning-by-inning, from reading off the teletype machine. Later they started doing broadcasts from visiting ballparks. Waite was so great at storytelling that they made a record album of his greatest stories.

Waite and his wife, Betty, joined us on a trip to Cooperstown, New York, for a visit to the National Baseball Hall of Fame where he was enshrined and many of his personal items were on display. We stayed at the beautiful, historic Otesaga Inn and after dinner, Waite entertained our group with many of his legendary tales. We continued on to Montreal where the Reds were playing the Expos in Olympic Stadium. We let the officials know that a Hall of Famer was in the crowd and they happily showed him on their Jumbo Tron screen. Waite was a well-educated man, an accomplished artist and a wonderful human being. He was a great friend.

Herb and Vada Pinson during Reds Dream Week, 1988.

Who's On Deck

In 1983 I met with Bill Bergesch, the Reds General Manager, to discuss the possibility of starting a Reds Cruise where players, broadcasters, managers, and coaches would be special guests and provide the opportunity for mingling with their fans. We chose to do the cruise in November, after the regular season, playoffs, and World Series. We came to an agreement and the Cincinnati Reds Cruise was born with Barney Rapp Travel operating the event. I even asked Marge Schott, the managing general partner, president and CEO of the Reds, to join us. She had one requirement. She wanted to bring her dog Schottzie with her. Of course that wasn't going to be possible, so she declined.

The first cruise started the tradition of having Reds radio broadcasters, Marty Brennaman and Joe Nuxhall, join us each year. Our first cruise was on the *Song of America* and also featured Jose Rio who, as an added surprise to all the fans, loved to sing Karaoke. Bill Bergesch who helped negotiate the cruise was also there and was referred to as "Dollar Bill." There was born a tradition and to this date the cruise departs each November with 2016's cruise being our 33rd annual!

Back row: Tom Browning, Barry Larkin, and John Franco. *Front Row:* Joe Nuxhall, Marty Brennaman, Eric Davis, and Danny Jackson.

After several years of being known as the Cincinnati Reds Cruise, we had to cancel our arrangement with the Reds. Marge Schott wanted more money to have the cruise be sponsored by the Reds, so we changed the name to the All-Star Baseball Cruise and Marty and Joe continued to sail with us each year. It became so popular with the fans that we had an eighty percent repeat factor from our guests, encouraging us to add to the name: All-Star Baseball Cruise and Reunion. For over thirty-two years we have sailed most of the Caribbean, the Mexican Riviera, and the Panama Canal. Players attending over the years included Tony Perez, Paul O'Neill, Eric Davis, Barry Larkin, Todd Frazier, Chris Sabo, Billy Hatcher, Hal Morris, Joe Oliver, Jack Billingham, Jim Maloney, Doug Flynn, Jeff Brantley, Brandon Phillips, Drew Stubbs, Ron

Oester, Billy Hatcher, John Franco, Danny Jackson, Brett Boone, Jose Rio, Lee May, Reggie Sanders, Buddy Bell, Billy Doran, and Ted Powers, just to name a few. Added to the cruise roster were managers Jack McKeon and our favorite, Sparky Anderson, who sailed with us eleven times. Marty has made all thirty-two of our cruises through 2015 and one of our passengers, Carol Hils, has also made every trip. We certainly miss Joe Nuxhall who sailed with us on every cruise until his death. He loved to hold court at about 4:00 in the afternoon, out at the deck bar, with a Heineken in hand, telling great stories. He was loved by all and we were on the cruise when we learned of his passing. We had a moment of silence for him on board and one of our passengers sang "Amazing Grace." Marty and Sparky told many stories about Joe. That cruise

Susie and Herb with Sparky Anderson.

certainly held our most somber experience. But, on the other side of the coin, we've had some very joyous occasions on our sailings too. Both Barry Larkin and Todd Frazier proposed with engagement rings to Lisa and Jackie, respectively, during cruises with us.

On one of our cruises to the Mexican Riviera, we stopped in Mazatlán, Mexico, where we heard about a place called Señor Frogs. Well, this was the first of many visits to other Frogs locations. As we entered the place we saw people dancing on top of chairs and tables. There was a conga line where shots of tequila were squirted in your mouth as you passed by one of the servers. Needless to say, no one was feeling any pain when it was time to go back to the ship. One young lady who was not part of our group had to be wheeled out of the place in a wheelbarrow to a taxi. On another cruise, we stopped in the Cancun Señor Frogs and at 11:00 a.m. we took over the place exclusively for our group. Several of our players and their wives went up on the stage and performed. There was a large tube suspended from the ceiling and if you wanted to shoot through the tube you had to climb a ladder, enter the tube and the water flow would shoot you out of the building into the Gulf of Mexico. Marty Brennaman purchased a swim suit, climbed the ladder, and went shooting out of the building while we all lined up at windows and watched this spectacular event taking place. He did a similar thing at the Señor Frogs in Aruba, this time in his tighty-whities. We have pictures to prove it!

During our Cancun stop we had to stop one of our motor coaches at a convenience store and purchase more beer. One of our guests, Ruth Cullen, walked from the back of the coach all the way to the front by using the aisle arm rests on which to walk. Always a great adventure, our special island parties are historical.

On a port stop to St. Lucia many of us headed for the beach. There was a boat giving parasailing rides. The Reds players with us on that trip were Tom Browning, Barry Larkin, John Franco, Danny Jackson, and Eric Davis.

They asked me to arrange for them to parasail. The man in charge said they were going to lunch and we would have to wait. Eric Davis extended his hand to him, his palm holding a $100 bill, and he asked him if lunch could wait. We immediately climbed in the boat. They called me the Air Commander and we all took a turn parasailing. Tom Browning and Danny Jackson flipped upside down while in the harness; real daredevils. Bill Bergesch saw this and almost had an attack on the shore. The players weren't supposed to participate in those types of activities!

Bill Bergesch was a wonderful man and he and his wife, Virginia, went on many of the baseball cruises. On one of our cruises to Grand Cayman, many of us decided to take a KonTiki cruise. Before we even set sail, the 150 proof rum punch was flowing. Joe Nuxhall kept adding more rum to the concoction, using his left hand to stir and update the elixir. The drink went down very smoothly, but after a short time we started feeling no pain. We returned to our ship and had to climb up a very long and steep gangway to reach the ship entrance. Bill Bergesch was having some difficulty climbing the stairs so we had to push him from behind till he reached the top. Once on board it was soon dinner time. We had made a pact that if any of us were unable to make it to dinner, there would be a cash penalty to pay. Shortly after arriving at dinner we looked around to see if everyone was there and there was no Bill Bergesch. No one was surprised, but about ten minutes later, who came wandering into the dining room as if he was on auto pilot? Bill. He never missed a meal.

Once, we were on the smallest Royal Caribbean ship, the *Sun Viking*. There were only about 400 passengers on board and our group took up 147 of that number. We practically owned the ship. The captain even had a private party for the players with a special cake depicting a baseball diamond. It was on this cruise that Barry asked Lisa to marry him and gave her a beautiful ring.

There were also many great entertainers on these cruises including Jerry Lewis, Norm Crosby, Al Martino, and Ben Vereen. On one cruise there was a show featuring a hypnotist who selected a group from the audience to be his subjects. Among this group was Reds outfielder Reggie Sanders, who appeared to be hypnotized as they had him running through the audience howling like a dog. The ship provided a video tape of the hypnotist show and it was played in the Reds clubhouse many times. Reggie claimed he didn't remember doing this. Another time two comedians had an act where they would juggle long-bladed knives and throw them back and forth to each other. They selected Billy Hatcher from the Reds to stand between them as they tossed these knives back and forth to each other. You should have seen the look on Billy's face as the blades passed back and forth near him. These were great moments to remember and we look forward to wonderful new memories every year.

The Rough Riders

The Reds moved their spring training camp to Sarasota in 1997. That first year during the week we attended, it rained for about three days. Game after game was canceled. We had to find other activities for the Rooters. A friend of ours who had moved to Sarasota recommended a casino boat that would do a gambling cruise from Venice, Florida. Vegas in Venice was preceded by a continental breakfast at the reception building and then a four-hour cruise in the Gulf of Mexico where after sailing out two miles, the casino would open.

We met with the owner and decided to do the cruise. The next day the weather cleared, yet there wasn't going to be a ballgame, so we took our entire group of over one hundred fifty to Venice for the cruise. After the continental breakfast, they would board the boat and sail away. While they were at breakfast, I walked out to the pier to see the boat and immediately realized that it wasn't as large as I was told it would be. Looking over the outside of the vessel, a man came up to me and asked if I was thinking of sailing on it. I told him we had a large group that was boarding in about thirty minutes for a cruise. He shook his head, called me crazy and asked if I had seen the size of the waves in the Gulf. It looked pretty calm to me right there, but we were in the protected cove and not outside of the break wall.

Sure enough, we boarded and sailed off and as soon as we cleared the protected area, I knew we were in big trouble. We started bouncing and rolling. It was unbelievable. It was like riding a mechanical bull at a western saloon. Many of the group immediately got sea sick, putting their heads down on the blackjack tables and lying on the floor. When they turned on the slot machines and those wheels started rolling, it was even worse. We had been out for about an hour when I found the captain to ask him to turn back. It was too rough to continue the cruise. He informed me that since we didn't charter the boat and he had other passengers on board, he was continuing the cruise.

I told our guests who weren't feeling well, which included me, to go up on the open top deck for some fresh air as that might help. Well, the water didn't get any smoother and everyone, not just our group, was complaining and urging the captain to turn back. Finally, he agreed to turn around. Unfortunately, it took us an hour and a half to get back to port.

Up on the top deck, many of us were sucking in the fresh air with deep breaths, which seemed to help. The trip back to port seemed to take forever and the waves seemed to get stronger. I was sitting in a light plastic chair holding onto a pole and not feeling great, but hoping to make it without being sick. Land was in sight when all of a sudden the boat hit a large wave, lurched sideways, and knocked me out of my seat. And, with that came a volume out of my mouth as if it had been fired from a cannon, hitting the person seated in front of me who was wearing a white jacket. Bullseye! Prior to sailing, at the continental breakfast, I had eaten a bagel, tomato juice, and strawberry yogurt. At first, I thought I was hemorrhaging internally, before I realized it was what I had earlier consumed. We threw away the jacket and I happily replaced it.

After disembarking the boat, I went looking for the owner to tell him we should have never been allowed to sail under those conditions, but, of course, he was long gone.

Show Business

On that same first trip to Sarasota we went to the Showboat, a dinner theatre in Clearwater. In addition to having a buffet dinner, you would then sit in the theater and see a show. The featured production playing that night was *Phantom of the Opera*. Many of our group had seen the Broadway production of Andrew Lloyd Weber's sensational show so the evening sounded great—dinner and the beautiful music and story of what took place in that Paris opera house.

After about thirty minutes into the show, we all realized that this production bore no likeness to the Broadway version and was really very amateur. We sat through the first act and finally made it to intermission. At the urging of many, we took a vote to see if we should leave before the next act began. One hundred percent voted to get out of there as fast as we could. Needless to say we practically emptied the theater, got back on the motor coaches, and left. You can imagine that when the curtain opened for act two, it was a real *phantom*, as most of the audience had disappeared.

Round and Round We Go

I have planned and escorted show and shopping trips to New York City, both in the spring and during the Christmas season, for many years. These trips included top Broadway shows, the Radio City Christmas Spectacular, city sightseeing, and restaurant meals. On one of the Christmas trips, I was approached to see if a group of about twenty elderly seniors could join our group. Since I had thirty people already booked, this would be a group within my group, which was fine. Whenever we attend a Broadway show, I always tell my group to stay seated until the theater is almost empty, as I will be waiting outside in front to direct them to the motor coach that will take them back to the hotel. Well, that didn't happen. This smaller group started coming out the main doors and were each heading in different directions, some going right, some left, and some going straight across the street. None of them were looking for me. I had to do the roundup, running after each one and bringing them back to wait for the rest of our group.

On Sunday morning, our final day of the trip, we headed for the Marriott Marquis Hotel which has a revolving restaurant at the top, featuring a fantastic Sunday brunch. To get to the top was a complicated ordeal. First, we entered on street level where there are about ten elevators in a circular configuration that must be taken up about six floors to the lobby level. Once successfully reaching the lobby and waiting for all fifty members of the group to ascend from different elevators and group together, we next needed to take two escalators to another level where a special elevator is used to reach the restaurant. It took several turns on this elevator to get the entire group to the top.

On arrival, we were met by a host who showed us the section where our tables were located. At this point, our group put their heavy winter coats on the wall hooks and proceeded to the buffet where they also had an omelet-to-order station. Now, being a revolving restaurant with a great view of Manhattan, when our guests finished getting their food, plates in hand, they couldn't find the tables where they were supposed to sit. The restaurant had moved. What a mess! I finally told them all to sit wherever they wanted because it was quite clear they were never going to figure out where we had been before. I headed back to our original section, got down on my hands and knees to look for purses, coats and other personal items that were left there, and tried to find the rightful owners of these objects. In the meantime, we were still revolving.

Once the brunch was over, we needed to leave to get back on the motor coach and head to Radio City Music Hall for the 11:00 a.m. Christmas Spectacular. After everyone found the restrooms and gathered their coats, I told them to go directly and immediately to the lower level and be prepared to depart right away. So, down to the lobby and on to the restaurant elevator, down two escalators and then to the street level via the ten elevators in front of us. After waiting for everyone to descend from the restaurant level, I made my way down to the street level and realized we were missing about half our group. Many of them had reached the lobby level, got on the wrong elevators and were whisked up and down to the hotel section floors. Ugh! We were twenty minutes from show time at Radio City. Finally, little by little, we secured the missing persons, got on the bus and just made it to the performance. What an adventure. I never used that restaurant again!

Hell No, We Won't Go

It seems some of my wildest experiences have been with radio station advertiser groups. On one occasion, after a delightful Southern Caribbean cruise, we headed for the San Juan airport for our flight to Atlanta and onward to Cincinnati. We arrived at the airport, stopped at the ticket counter to obtain our boarding passes and check our luggage. Everything was going like clockwork until we were informed that our flight was delayed due to mechanical problems. Our departing plane had not even made it to San Juan yet. It was still grounded, three hours away, at another airport.

On days when cruises come into port, the San Juan airport is packed and there are very few places to sit, especially for a three or four-hour wait. The airlines offered us vouchers to use as cash for airport food but the amount wasn't much. I suggested that they allow our group of forty-six the use of their private lounge. At first the answer was a negative. Being a Sunday, they said the lounge was already closed. This was unacceptable, so I insisted and was able to encourage them to open the lounge just for our group.

They sent a very young man to unlock the door for us and in we went. Then things started to get interesting. Several of our group members took over the bar, even sending the young man for more beverages, as the inventory on hand was quickly depleted. Everyone was having a good time and didn't seem at all upset about the flight delay.

The drinks were flowing, the spirits were high, and the television behind the bar was broadcasting the final round of the Masters Tournament in Augusta. As the leading contenders approached hole number eighteen, locked in a tie, the announcement came that our flight had arrived and we were to proceed to the gate for immediate boarding. Well, with the large consumption of adult beverages and the exciting conclusion to the golf tournament, I couldn't get anyone to move. I announced again

Jim Mogan and Herb—off the clock.

that we needed to go and almost in unison the chanting began, "Hell no, we won't go." It took a great effort but with the help of the airline staff we finally got everyone out of the lounge and down to the gate for boarding the aircraft.

Once on board and seated, it was clear there were only a few other passengers other than our group on the plane. Our group started asking the flight attendants for more drinks, which after looking at the condition of our group, they considerately refused. After takeoff, the group settled down and many of our passengers fell asleep for the duration of the flight. One of our gentlemen was dead to the world and had his feet resting on top of the empty seat in front of him. This provided the opportunity for one of our ladies to paint his toenails different colors while he was sleeping. When he later woke up, he looked like the NBC peacock. What a way to end the trip. Luckily I have a lot of this on my video camera. It's well worth watching!

Lemons

When the Red Rooters traveled to Los Angeles to see games at Dodger Stadium, we always stayed downtown at the historic Biltmore hotel. The sales manager for all of the major professional sports teams, including the Reds, was Andy Martin. He was a character and he loved Barney Rapp and the Rooters. Andy would greet us as we arrived and hand out the room keys. He always had a trick or gimmick. On one occasion, he approached our group with the sound of a phone ringing from his jacket pocket (this was decades before cell phones). He reached inside his jacket pocket, producing a telephone receiver and immediately put it to his ear. He said a few words into the receiver and then handed it to me as he nodded, "Here, it's for you." What a gag! I knew I had to have one of those ringing receivers and play the joke forward, and I did.

Andy and his wife, Joyce, once joined us on a trip to Europe. Andy loved lemons. He put lemon on everything, squeezed the juice out of them until they were dry. He couldn't get enough. On our river cruise the ship was actually running out of lemons, so when we stopped along the way, we had to go to local markets and purchase more. On our arrival at the Palace Hotel in Lucerne, Switzerland, we decided to play a trick on Andy. We obtained a dozen lemons and while he was out of his room, we snuck in and put lemons under his mattress, in his pillows and in the covers. The next morning when we saw him, he asked to have his room changed complaining that his mattress and bedding were terribly uncomfortable. He said he didn't get any sleep because the bed was lumpy and he couldn't find a comfortable position all night. Then he continued, "I hope they have enough lemons in the kitchen." As you can imagine, we burst out laughing. We finally told him that we had put his favorite citrus fruit near to him and followed up by presenting him the receipt for the lemons we purchased. At first he didn't think it was very funny, but he later grew to appreciate the trick we played on him and he loved it. He was a good sport!

You Won't Believe This

It all started when a group of thirty-six of us left for a Mediterranean cruise with 700-WLW's Jim Scott and his wife Donna. We left Cincinnati for Atlanta and had a four-hour layover until our flight to Rome. Upon our arrival in Rome, we cleared customs and waited for our luggage at the carousel. We waited and waited, and waited, until the belt stopped and there were no more suitcases coming through. Nineteen of us were missing our luggage. Next stop: Baggage Service Office, where we had to individually make claims for all of our missing luggage. It took quite some time to fill out all the appropriate paperwork and we were supposed to be starting on a Rome city tour, including a visit to the Vatican and Sistine Chapel. In the meantime, I called our office in Cincinnati to have them track the missing luggage. We eventually filed all the claims, did our city tour, and then went to Civitavecchia (the port for Rome) to board our ship, most of us with just what we had been wearing since the time we left home more than twenty hours earlier.

Our ship, the *Royal Princess* sailed that evening for our first port of call, Sorrento, Italy. We all went to dinner that evening wearing what we had on, some of our group in shorts. My office informed me that our luggage was still in Atlanta! Even though Delta had four hours during our layover, for some reason they didn't get the bags on our flight. Delta assured my office that the luggage would be put on the next flight to Rome that evening and it would arrive in Rome the next morning. Since we already had left Rome, my contact there was going to collect the luggage, put it on a truck and send it down to Sorrento where it would be put on our ship. Everyone seemed okay with that. After all, things happen, right?

The next morning we anchored in Sorrento. My group was scheduled to take a tour to Pompeii followed by lunch in Sorrento. I decided to wait for the luggage to arrive and get it on board our ship. The group left for the tour and I called my agent in

Herb in Cairo, Egypt, visiting the Great Pyramids.

Rome to see if they had secured the luggage. Guess what? The luggage wasn't on the plane. This was a substantial problem because the ship would be sailing for two days until we reached our next port, Alexandria, Egypt. The group returned from their tour and met me at the restaurant. I had to deliver the bad news that we were probably not going to see our luggage until we got to Cairo in three days. After lunch, I told everyone to shop at the few stores that were open on Sunday to purchase whatever they could find and keep the receipts.

When we boarded our ship, the staff was very concerned for us and graciously offered a gift shop merchandise credit so we could buy any items that we needed. They also offered free laundry service until we were reunited with our luggage. That was a very nice gesture, as it was the airlines fault the luggage never arrived. After another day, I received news that our luggage would be waiting for us in Cairo. As mentioned, our next port was Alexandria, Egypt, which was a three-hour drive to Cairo. The shore excursion agent on our ship informed us that all of us that had missing luggage had to be taken to the Cairo airport to identify and secure their luggage and, as a result of the necessary time required to travel to the airport, those members of our group wouldn't have time to visit the pyramids. Can you imagine coming all this way and not seeing one of the main attractions of our cruise?

Luckily, most of our group had selected an optional tour for an overnight stay at a Four Seasons Hotel in Cairo that included a sound and light show at the pyramids and a Nile

River breakfast cruise before continuing the next day to where our ship had been repositioned in Port Said, Egypt. I arranged for those members of our group that had not signed up, to be added onto the overnight to insure we all could see the pyramids. We went to the airport and there on a large cart was our missing luggage. Hooray! We collected our bags and headed to our hotel to clean up, change clothes, and enjoy a great evening and breakfast cruise before taking our long drive to rejoin our ship in Port Said.

On our arrival in Port Said, we were welcomed back on board and our luggage was sent to our cabins. Time to set sail to our next port: Haifa, Israel. It looked like things were getting a lot better—not so. We had just left port and were ready for dinner when the ship's alarm sounded with the dreaded seven-short and one-long blast. An announcement quickly followed that informed us that there was a fire on board the ship. We were instructed to get our life vests and proceed to our muster stations. Our station was the Main Lounge and en route you could smell smoke. We gathered in a very warm room; no power, no air conditioning and of course we hadn't had dinner. Hot and hungry! Since the power was off they kept making progress announcements over a bullhorn. They passed out sandwiches, fruit, and drinks. If anyone needed to use the restroom, they were escorted up four flights of stairs and entered a dark restroom, hoping that everything would be all right in the pitch darkness.

After our confinement in the lounge for several hours, we were finally permitted to go up to the pool deck and stretch out on the deck furniture. In the near distance we could see the lights of Port Said and other ships near us. We were dead in the water, watching the hours slowly tick by. At about 4:00 a.m. we were allowed to return to our cabins. There was no electricity except for some emergency lighting in the hall, so we kept our cabin doors open to allow for some light.

The next morning we were told that we were going to be towed back to Port Said where inspectors would board to inspect the damage from the fire. We spent all day in port with power supplied from the pier. We could get off and go into town if we desired. That evening while at dinner, the captain made an announcement that the fire had been in the engine room and the damage was so severe that our ship couldn't continue the voyage. The cruise was to be discontinued. We further were told that Princess Cruise representatives would be on board the next morning giving us information and air tickets for our return home. Our cruise fare was to be fully refunded, plus we would all receive a credit voucher for a future cruise on Princess. I rushed down to the ship's office and told them I wanted to make certain that our group would all be on the same flights back home.

The next morning I was first in line waiting for the representatives. I was given our flight information and found that they had split our group into three different flights. I was assigned with some of our group to fly home via Paris, Jim Scott and Donna with some through Amsterdam, and one of our seasoned travelers would lead the group home from Istanbul.

Late that evening, we boarded our motor coaches for the three-hour ride back to the Cairo airport and boarded our different flights to Paris, Amsterdam, or Istanbul. Well, we all made it home, surviving lost luggage, a ship fire, and the remainder of the cruise being canceled.

It took me several months to file claims for the missing luggage, the purchase of needed items reimbursement, ship refund, air tickets, and more.

I have to say that this was the worst experience I ever encountered on a trip I escorted, but everyone returned home safely and had great stories to recount from this trip.

By the way, most of the group took a similar trip with us the following year and, fortunately, we made it to Israel without any consequences.

The Weather Outside is Frightful

One of the biggest lessons of traveling: Always be prepared for Mother Nature. We've learned we can't do anything about the weather. I had a group from a television station in Mobile, Alabama, that traveled to Switzerland during some very heavy rain showers throughout Europe. We arrived in Lucerne to find the lake was flooded and way over its shoreline. There had been enormous storms for days and flooding was everywhere. You couldn't take a lakeside stroll because the water was all the way up to the lakefront side of the building. Some of the main streets of Lucerne were closed to traffic due to flooding and many of the places we were scheduled to visit were impassable. So, we made the best of it by creating alternate plans to enjoy Switzerland. We got to see many things we probably wouldn't have seen in the best of weather, so it turned out well. We had a great experience getting to these places and had a wonderful time once we got there.

It once again seemed as if our complication was resolved, until we got news from home that a massive hurricane was heading to Mobile. The foreboding weather forecast meant that many members of our group had to get back home quickly. Their focus became to return to Mobile and protect their homes and businesses that possibly would be in the path of the storm. I learned later that several who left early and flew through Atlanta had to rent cars and vans to drive to Mobile, as the airport there had already been closed.

On other trips including two European river cruises, we were faced, one year, with the river being very low due to lack of rain and then the next year another river being too high with a very swift current which prevented us from sailing. We didn't miss a thing, lived on the boat, and were taken by motor coach to see all of the sites.

You never know what you may be faced with when you travel, but you need to be ready to make alternative decisions no matter what comes your way. Fortunately, after forty-three years of experiencing a variety of situations, our outcomes have always been successful.

We Paid for It

Vietnam was opened to tourists and we had a group on board the *Sun Viking* for a ten-day cruise from Hong Kong to include ports in Vietnam, Thailand, and Singapore. Early on, we couldn't help but notice two of the passengers on board: a woman pushing a man in a wheelchair who we found out was her husband. We saw both of them frequently during the first days of the cruise, in port and around the ship. After a few days of cruising, we kept seeing the woman but observed she was now always by herself. We wondered where her husband might be. Curiosity got the best of us, so we inquired with one of the cruise staff. They told us that he had died. That was not the answer we expected. However, the shocking part came next. We were told that even though her husband had died, the wife had stayed on the cruise, declaring, "We paid for this trip and we are going to finish it." We then asked the obvious question as to where the deceased husband might be and were told he was down below in a special refrigeration unit and would remain there until we arrived at our last port. You never know!

Don't Jump

I did several trips with Nick and Nina Clooney. They had a wonderful following of fans and were great hosts. On a trip to Hawaii, we were staying at the Kauai Marriott Resort. I had a room on the top floor about ten stories high with a large balcony. It was a beautiful afternoon and I decided to sit out on my balcony and enjoy the amazing site of the sun setting over the Pacific Ocean.

I went out on the balcony and closed my glass sliding door so the air conditioner would stay on. After a while I got up to go back in my room and to my astonishment the door had locked. The only way to get the door open was from inside the room. I saw a group of people ten stories below on the lawn and started shouting and waving to get their attention. They looked up and not being close enough to hear my pleas of help, they just kept waving back trying to be friendly. I hope they didn't think I was going to jump off. This plan was clearly not going to work. Now what to do?

I suddenly realized that I had my cell phone in my pocket. Although I didn't have any local numbers in my phone, I called my wife Susie who was back in Cincinnati. I told her to call the hotel and have them send someone to my room to unlock the sliding door, letting me back in my room. After what seemed like an hour, I was free, safe and sound inside my room. Luckily, I had my phone. Otherwise I'm not sure how long I would have been stranded. This memory has stayed with me and has become a constant fear. Now, every time I go out on a balcony, I am careful to not close the door all the way.

I told Nick Clooney about what happened to me. Since he wrote a newspaper column for the *Cincinnati Post*, he was happy to embellish the story of the "locked out group leader." It was printed for all to read once we arrived home.

What's Poppin'

Located in Spain on the beautiful Mediterranean is the Costa del Sol. I was with a group on our final stop of visiting Portugal and Spain when I noticed the familiar Rotary sign at our hotel, indicating that the Rotary Club would meet there that evening. I was a member from the Cincinnati Club which was among the first clubs to be established. It was customary when visiting another club to introduce yourself and exchange flags from each club.

I hadn't any plans that evening so I decided to attend. After the meeting the president of the club came up to me and asked if I could meet him the next day. I was intrigued as to why he wanted to meet with me, but I agreed to find him in the lobby at noon. Upon meeting, he explained that he had several convenience stores and that each store had a popcorn machine manufactured by Gold Medal Products in Cincinnati. He went on to explain that he still owed Gold Medal for some of the machines that were shipped to him and asked, since I lived in Cincinnati, if I would take payment back for his account. He handed me an envelope that held $5,000 in U.S. cash currency.

I told him I couldn't take it. "I don't want the responsibility," I sputtered, "and you don't know me well enough to trust me with that amount of money!" He responded stalwartly, "I trust you. You are a Rotarian." I was very nervous about this but after a bit more convincing, I took the envelope. The next day we left on our flight back home. I held on tightly to that envelope as if it was attached to me permanently.

The day after we arrived back home, I drove down to the offices of Gold Medal Products and asked to see the treasurer. I had such a feeling of relief as I handed off the envelope with the $5,000. I requested a receipt, just in case, and explained how I got involved in transporting the funds. He smiled and told me that I wasn't the first person to bring them payment from their client. Really? This had happened before? He asked me to wait a moment and returned carrying two large bags of unpopped corn kernels. That was my reward for bringing them the payment. To this day, every time I go to a movie theater or any place where popcorn is served, I'm reminded of this incident and have to pause for just a moment to smile.

Hold On

We took many wonderful river cruises on the *Delta Queen,* *Mississippi Queen,* and *American Queen* steamboats. On a cruise out of Cincinnati to New Orleans, my wife, Susie, and daughter, Julianne, were the escorts for our Cincinnati group. I had been on another trip but upon returning, I decided to surprise them by showing up at the New Orleans landing as the boat arrived. I could see the boat coming down the Mississippi River so I quickly left the hotel and walked toward the nearby landing. As I approached the roadway leading to the landing, I was prevented from going further as the way was blocked by a very long, stationary, freight train. I anxiously awaited the train's movement so I could cross the tracks and meet the boat as it arrived. With no movement in sight, I finally made the decision to duck under the train car. Just as I got up my courage to make a run for it, the train started to roll. That wouldn't have been a very good move. Whew!

After several minutes, all the cars had made their way down the tracks and the roadway was clear. I made it to the boat just as the gangway was set. I went up the gangway and into the lobby where I found Susie and Julianne helping the group get ready to disembark the boat. With very little welcome or surprise in seeing me, they were entrenched in the business at hand, so I thought I'd get to work, as well. One of their passengers was a

Herb's daughter, Julianne, and son, Steve.

man in a wheelchair and I was directed to take him down the gangway to the bottom of the landing. The gangway off the boat was very steep, probably about a forty-five-degree slope. I started down, holding on firmly to the wheelchair. Unexpectedly, gravity took over and the chair felt like I was holding on to an elephant. I thought surely I was going to lose my grip which would cause the chair and the passenger to end up in the river. "Put on the brakes," I yelled! I wrapped my leg around one of the rail supports and hollered for help. We fortunately regained control and made it safely down to the flat dock area. So much for surprising my wife and daughter!

Baby It's Cold Inside

Back in 1967, before I got into this business, I had a couple of weeks free before starting a new job. Susie and I decided to take a road trip to Montreal, Canada, to visit Expo '67. It was early April and the Expo had just opened. Barney Rapp had put together a tour to Expo '67 later that summer so our timing was perfect to check out the site and see where the group was going to be staying.

Packed up in our station wagon, we arrived in Montreal, ready to check out the accommodations and report back to Barney. It took quite a bit of searching to find the place where the group would stay that summer and where we planned to stay during our trip. Imagine our dismay when we found that the overnight lodging was actually temporary units that had been built for the duration of the Expo. Even worse, many of the fabricated units were not yet completed. We parked in a muddy lot, found the office, and were given the key to our room with directions on where to park. When we tried driving up to our unit, we got stuck in the mud. The tires were spinning and spinning. Not a good start to our scouting mission. It was no use. We finally had to get a wrecker to pull us out of the muck. The fun wasn't over. April in Montreal is still pretty cold, and once we reached our room, it felt like walking into a refrigerator. We looked for the thermostat only to discover the heater wasn't connected. It was late, so we decided we could stick it out for the night. Staying fully dressed, we climbed into bed, covered ourselves in blankets, cuddled up, and hoped our chattering teeth wouldn't keep us awake. It certainly wasn't the relaxing vacation we had planned. Even a trip to the bathroom was an adventure because the toilet had a metal seat. This created some exciting new posture positions!

As you might have guessed, the very next day we checked out and went to a hotel. We were committed to making the rest of our trip a success and it was. Expo '67 was fantastic. And when the group did arrive later in July, those temporary buildings where we first stayed were finally completed and were very nice and, thankfully, very cozy.

Bing-Bang

Some tours become absolutely unforgettable once it sinks in just how lucky you were to be there. We did a trip to the British Isles with a first stop in London. Included in our itinerary was a performance at the famed London Palladium. The group was unaware of where we were going or who we were going to see perform. It was all a well-kept secret. To everyone's amazement, we had tickets to see Bing Crosby. Bing had recently started performing again as he had previously hurt himself during a stage fall and had canceled many of his shows. He was accompanied on stage by his wife Kathryn, their son, and special guest Rosemary Clooney. It was a terrific show and we all enjoyed the special treat of seeing the great Bing Crosby and Rosemary Clooney together on stage. It was like watching a scene from the movie *White Christmas*, but in real life.

About a week later while continuing on our trip, we were all in Scotland at Edinburgh castle when we received word that Bing Crosby had died while on a golf course in Spain. Of course this was a great shock to all of us. We remarked how fortunate we were to have seen him in one of his last few performances. This is something we will never forget.

Weekend Warriors

For many years, we operated both Red Rooter and Bengals weekends in Cincinnati. During the Big Red Machine years we would have five hundred to seven hundred guests arrive at our downtown hotel on a Friday afternoon, attend our hospitality party, and then go to Riverfront Stadium for the night game. On Saturday, tacked on to the afternoon or night game, we had a dinner buffet with six serving lines followed by a festive party. The celebration included a live band playing late into the evening and all the beer and snacks that one desired. Reds fans would come from little towns all over Ohio, Kentucky, Indiana, and West Virginia. We even had a couple who loved Reds baseball and traveled from Japan to join us. It was such a thrill to spend the weekend enjoying the Reds winning game after game. The most popular weekends were when the Dodgers, Giants, and Cardinals were in for a three-game series. It felt like the festivities never stopped. At the Saturday night after-game parties, table after table was stacked high with empty beer cans. Then to top off the weekend on Sunday, we served a sit down breakfast before everyone left for the afternoon game. Those were great days!

The Red Rooters at a game.

Our football weekends were quite different. Besides starting on Saturday afternoons, originally, we would send the fans via motor coach to the Beverly Hills Supper Club in Kentucky for dinner and a wonderful show featuring top entertainers. Then on Sunday morning, we included a breakfast at the hotel and a ticket to the afternoon football game at Riverfront Stadium.

After the tragic fire at Beverly Hills Supper Club, things changed. We still had the guests arrive at our hotel on Saturday, but instead hosted a cocktail party and dinner that night, followed by the breakfast and game on Sunday. Usually we had upwards of one hundred tickets for each game. It wasn't always just Bengals fans that enjoyed these weekends. A tavern owner in

Pittsburgh assembled a group that would travel four-and-a-half hours by motor coach for the Bengals-Steelers game each year.

One of those years their coach arrived in the early evening and the group began unloading cases of Iron City beer to take into the hotel. They were all pretty well tipsy and before taking the time to check into their rooms, they immediately wanted to know where the cocktail party was being held. Observing their highly intoxicated condition, I told them we would have drinks with the brunch on Sunday and that they didn't need any more alcohol that night. Well, as you can imagine, they didn't seem to like that answer and literally backed me into a corner where I feared for my life. Here was a swarm of big iron workers from Pittsburgh looking to work me over if they didn't get their way. I panicked and started yelling for security. Finally, I was relieved of this precarious situation and vowed to never find myself in a perilous position like that again. Needless to say, I quit including groups from Pittsburgh in our football weekends, although their fans have shown up in huge numbers at those games and still do.

Don't Miss the Boat

The anxiety of knowing some of your guests are not on-board the ship as it prepares to sail has, unnervingly, happened twice. The first was on a Mediterranean cruise where we were in the port of Dubrovnik, Croatia. On this particular ship they had a system in place that assigned each passenger a number. Upon disembarking the ship at each port, guests passed a board near the gangway entrance that contained a little disc with numbers hanging from a board. Each passenger took their number off the hook and carried it with them. This way, when returning to the ship, the number could be hung back on the designated space and the crew would know everyone was back on board. Obviously, this was before the electronic way they do it now. Well, the ship was getting ready to sail and two numbers were missing from the board. Of course, the absent passengers were part of my group. They made an announcement over the ship's public address system calling for the two passengers, without any response. The ships officer contacted me to report that they were ready to sail and unfortunately the two missing passengers would have to fly to our next port to rejoin the ship.

Earlier, I had seen the two missing ladies in Dubrovnik waiting for the shuttle bus which would bring them back to the ship. I requested that the ship delay departure so I could take a taxi back to town to look for the ladies. That wasn't an option the crew was interested in and just as they started to move the stairs to the gangway, I saw a taxi pull up. The two ladies got out of the cab and slowly began to meander towards our ship. I shouted to them to hurry up and get on board as we were ready to sail! Once safely aboard the ship, they explained they hadn't changed their watches to the local time and thought they still had an hour to get back. "Are we really getting ready to sail?" they asked. I told them to turn around and they immediately saw we had already casted off from the pier.

Another time, I had a group of about forty advertisers from a television station in Wichita, Kansas. It was mid-January and the perfect time to fly to Miami, Florida, for a week's voyage in the Caribbean. I received an early morning call on the day of the trip to inform me that the weather in Wichita was dreadful. Due to the extreme snow and ice, their flight to Miami was canceled. I immediately got on the phone with our air department and found another flight that would take them to Atlanta and then on to West Palm Beach, Florida. This would at least get them to Florida; however, it was seventy-five miles from the airport in West Palm Beach to the pier in Miami. It seemed almost impossible that they would get to Miami in time for the ship's sailing, but it was the only option, so I gave it a shot. Without further ado, I arranged for a motor coach to pick them up at the airport and drive them to the pier, normally a one-and-a-half hour trip.

I flew out of Cincinnati and upon arriving at the ship terminal, I explained the situation to the person in charge and asked if they would delay the sailing so the group could make it to the ship. They said they would wait only a half hour, as the ship had to sail to make the schedule. I took my luggage to my cabin but didn't dare unpack. If the group didn't make it in time I wasn't going to sail by myself for a whole week. Phone in hand, I stayed in contact with the group and heard they made it to Atlanta, then they flew to West Palm Beach. On arrival in West Palm Beach, I instructed them to grab their luggage, get on the motor coach, and rush to Miami.

As I stood in the terminal, I watched all of the reservation stations close one by one. The once bustling check-in area was now only occupied by a few baggage handlers. I stood by the gangway entrance with my luggage, ready to get off the ship in case they didn't make it. I kept getting reports via telephone of their progress. "They have to be close by," I thought. In order to keep the ship from sailing, I felt like I should hire a row boat and station myself in front of the ship, like the people in China did in Tiananmen Square in front of the tanks. The purser kept asking where the group was. Finally, I got a call that they were in sight of the ship. Whew! They arrived and immediately were brought on board with their luggage and I greeted each one of them with a big hug. Several asked if we would be sailing soon but before they could turn around, the door closed and we were slowly pulling out of port. The motor coach driver, I was told, had really put the pedal to the metal to get them there on time. What a close call!

Surprise Package

We were in Paris, the beautiful "City of Lights," and our group was on a tour of the city with stops at the various places of interest. At one of our stops we got off of the motor coach and walked over to the Trocadero, the beautiful area on the Seine River with a fantastic view of the Eiffel Tower; the best place to take pictures of this iconic monument. While we assembled on this site and listened to our guide for an explanation of the history of Gustave Eiffel and his dream of building this fabulous structure, we were encountered by a group of ambitious vendors demonstrating some type of a little bird toy that they repeatedly tossed in the air, forcing us to look up in wonderment at the little flying objects.

Strapped over our shoulders, we all had the red Barney Rapp Travel flight bags that were issued to everyone in the group. Our bags were filled with cameras, film, snacks and other personal items. My wife Susie had her wallet and other valuables in her bag and, regrettably, didn't have it zipped shut. We kind of shooed away these pesky fellows, boarded the coach, and off we went to our next stop: Notre-Dame Cathedral.

After spending sometime visiting the magnificent structure and thinking about the story of Quasi Moto the hunchback, we were cut loose for some time to shop at the souvenir stands adjacent to the Cathedral. Susie found some tee shirts and when she reached into her flight bag for her wallet, a sudden expression of fear came across her face; her wallet was gone! The wallet contained her driver's license, cash, and American Express traveler's checks. She was now in panic mode.

The next stop for the group was to be lunch up on Montmartre, the artist area where the Sacra Corer Church also was located. Susie and I immediately took a taxi to the American Express office near our hotel and told the group we would meet them at the restaurant. Fortunately, we had the numbers of the American Express checks that weren't cashed and in a very short time we were issued new ones. Somewhat relieved, but without her wallet, we rejoined the group for lunch. After warning everyone to be mindful of their belongings, the rest of the trip was uneventful.

Flash forward to about three months later. We received a letter on Paris police stationery, written in French. I gave the letter to our daughter Julie to take to her French high school teacher to translate. The letter stated that they had found Susie's wallet with her driver's license and if we wanted it returned, we needed to wire some money to take care of the postage. We sent off the payment and waited, wondering what would be in the wallet when we saw it again.

About a month later a small box arrived from France. Reminiscent of the father in *A Christmas Story* who received that huge box containing his winning prize, we excitedly and furiously ripped open the container. Guess what we found? There in the box was Susie's stolen wallet, her driver's license and, believe it or not, five other empty wallets of various shapes and sizes. Perhaps we were the only ones to actually reply to the police and send money for postage, so they sent us all of the wallets they had in their possession.

We Have Cooties

Jim Mogan and I escorted a group trip to New York City where we stayed at the Roosevelt Hotel. We returned from a city tour, and got on the elevator heading for our rooms to find it filled with people wearing funny-looking red hats. As the elevator traveled upward to our destination, we were informed that these red-hatted friendly folks called themselves Cooties. Straightaway, they invited us to join them in their party suite. We went to our rooms, refreshed, and headed up to their suite. We weren't sure if we needed to get some bug spray to protect ourselves from what sounded like a convention for pest exterminators.

Upon entering the room, we found a huge crowd of men and women, all wearing those silly looking red hats. We were immediately handed a drink, and from that moment on, the food and drinks kept coming our way. We were treated like one of the gang, except we didn't have red hats. We found out that they were a branch of the national Military Order of Cootie, a branch of the Veterans of Foreign Wars of the United States. The veterans' services organization was formed in New York City in 1920 with the purpose of bringing smiles and entertainment to hospitalized troops and social programs to the VFW. This was a very special treat for us and we learned something new about a wonderful and honorable organization that not only has fun, but does so much for our veterans. You never know who you might meet in an elevator.

The Hall

When Johnny Bench was elected to be inducted into the National Baseball Hall of Fame in 1989, we knew we were going to have a large contingent of Reds fans wanting to go to Cooperstown, New York, in July for the ceremony. Late January, Jim Mogan and I drove to Cooperstown, first stopping in Buffalo, Syracuse, and Rochester, New York, to scout out hotels and restaurants. Our plan for the induction trip was to start out from Cincinnati via motor coach and spend the night in Buffalo. We would continue the next day with an overnight in either Syracuse or Rochester which allowed us to leave early the next morning to get to Cooperstown. There wouldn't be any hotels in or near Cooperstown to take care of the large group we assumed would be with us.

On arriving in Cooperstown, Jim and I had to find a place where we could park a large number of motor coaches, get tickets to the Hall of Fame museum, provide lunches for the group, and after the induction ceremony, get back on the coaches. We also had to find hotels where our group could stay on the way back home to Cincinnati.

1990 World Series in Oakland.

Joe Nuxhall, Susie, and Marty Brennaman.

Joe Nuxhall and Susie.

We found a gas station on the corner of the main street of Cooperstown, near the museum, that could park a large number of our coaches. We paid in advance and reserved the whole lot. We found a caterer who would make bag lunches and arranged for these to be picked up by our guests at a downtown real estate office.

We left Cincinnati with approximately seven hundred Red Rooters, stayed overnight in Buffalo, continued on to the next hotels, provided breakfast, lunch, and dinners, and arrived in Cooperstown. In addition we had a group that was in Montreal seeing the Reds vs. the Expos. They joined us by motor coach in Cooperstown and flew back home after the ceremony.

The coordination was seamless and all worked well, except the induction, which then was held at the Hall of Fame library garden. The enormous crowd also included Boston Red Sox fans that came to see Carl Yastrzemski be inducted and the mass amount of both Reds and Red Sox fans couldn't fit into the limited space. Years later, they moved the induction ceremony to a new facility, capable of holding thousands of fans. Several years later, we repeated this process when Sparky Anderson, Marty Brennaman, and Tony Perez were inducted, and later Barry Larkin. The amount of coordination and early planning is absolutely necessary to avoid any problems for a successful trip.

Rubbing Elbows

Quite often, the large cruise lines invite travel agencies, media, and others to the naming of a new ship. On one extraordinary occasion in 1990, my wife Susie and I were invited to the official naming of the Princess Cruise line's new ship, the *Crown Princess*.

We flew to New York City and boarded the ship at Pier 34 on the Hudson River. After settling in our cabin, we were invited to the centrum of the ship for a special ceremony. After enjoying passed champagne and canapés, we were brought to attention by the blast of several trumpets, heralding us to bring our attention to the top of the main staircase. Standing there in a stunning gold colored gown was Sophia Loren, accompanied by her husband, the famous film director Carlo Ponti. They descended the staircase and the entire assembly of people, including us, were absolutely astonished as this beautiful woman radiantly appeared before us. She would be the Godmother of this ship.

After a delightful dinner we were invited to the theater for a show. We were sitting, waiting for the surprise entertainer, and were seated next to a very nice couple. After making small talk with our seat mates, we discovered that we were sitting next to

James Michener, the famous author. Finally, the lights dimmed. The orchestra started a swelling introduction and out came Tony Bennett to perform a forty-five minute show.

After the show we went up to the casino and standing next to me was Robin Leach, the star of the television show *Lifestyles of the Rich and Famous*. It truly was an evening of champagne and caviar.

Through the night, the ship had sailed over to the Brooklyn side of the Hudson. The next day, the passengers disembarked the ship and were taken by motor coaches to bleacher-type stands, given special seat cushions, and took seats facing the ship. After a short time, four white magnificent horses came into view pulling behind them a beautiful white, open carriage carrying Sophia Loren, Carlo Ponti, and the ship's captain. They exited the carriage at the bow of the ship where Sophia climbed a staircase which brought her closer to the ship. With a large pair of scissors in hand, she cut a ribbon which caused an enormous bottle of champagne to swing loose, crashing into the vessel and officially christening the *Crown Princess*.

This two-day adventure will absolutely go down as one of my greatest star-filled memories.

Foreign Relations

America has always been known as a melting pot. That could not be truer for many of us whose parents, grandparents, and even earlier generations came to this country from other distant lands. As I mentioned in my introduction, my father and grandparents on both sides of my family came from Europe early in the twentieth century.

Around 2001, I received a letter addressed from a Benjamin Reisenfeld living in Liege, Belgium. I eagerly tore it open, wondering who this mysterious person could possibly be. The letter indicated that this man lived with his wife, daughters, son, grandchildren, and sister in Belgium. His son Alain worked in the National Library in Brussels and had gone online to search for the family Reisenfeld. Provided with Alain's fruitful research, Benjamin had sent letters out to all the Reisenfelds he could find, detailing his father's past and emigration to Belgium from Poland in the 1920s. I never heard my father speak of this family so being curious I called the number listed in the letter.

I spoke to Jeanette, Benjamin's wife, who spoke better English, and I was able to learn more about their family. Knowing

I was going to be in Paris with a group a few weeks later, I asked how far Liege was from Paris. I learned that if I traveled on the high speed train from Paris, I could arrive in Liege in about two hours. My interest was sparked and there was no turning back. I told them I would come to Liege to meet them. I was excited to find out more about these other Reisenfelds.

The day finally arrived and I boarded the train from Paris. I had no idea what to expect, so my nerves were on edge. What would the day ahead bring? On arrival in Liege, I got off the train and found a woman waiting on the platform, holding a sign with my name. She greeted me and took me to their car where her brother Benjamin was waiting. This woman was Malvena, Benjamin Reisenfeld's sister. We continued to his home which was a beautiful apartment overlooking the river. Arriving at his building I stared in awe at the mailbox that listed the Reisenfeld name. It was such an odd feeling as I didn't know of that many Reisenfelds anywhere in the world, especially any still living in Europe.

Upon entering their apartment I was met and warmly welcomed by about twenty members of their family. Gazing at these strangers for the first time, I was astonished to see some resemblance to other members of my family. After our initial greetings, we all sat down to a sumptuous meal. It was an incredibly remarkable experience. Then the door opened and more family members entered. I felt like a much honored guest. We traded books—mine about Cincinnati and theirs about Liege. I found out that for centuries Liege was famous for manufacturing weapons and that the city was adjacent to the Argonne Forest where in WWII the Battle of the Bulge was fought.

I was so intrigued by their history. I asked how the family had survived during the war years and during the Holocaust. They told me that the women had all left Belgium to live in a farmhouse near the French border. The men were being taken away to serve as labor by the Nazis, but miraculously managed to escape during a train transport. They were able to make their way to where the rest of the family was hiding, and to avoid capture they hid away in the cellar of the farmhouse. When neighbors would inquire, the women simply explained that the men were away working. Then, during Christmas and other holidays, the men dressed up, came out of hiding and pretended to be Christians, only to go back into hiding immediately after the holiday. When they had heard that the American Army had arrived in Europe, they hoped it was safe to return to Liege. However, on arriving home they saw that a mighty battle was being fought in the Argonne so they had to go back in hiding for a while longer.

After hearing this story and quizzing each other about our families, I felt there was definitely some connection between us. We accepted with hugs and kisses that we certainly must be cousins. I was ready to go back to my hotel, exhausted physically from the journey and mentally from the emotional experience, when I was told we were going to sit down for dinner. I thought that is what we had done when I first arrived. I was given a seat of honor next to Benjamin. Both my heart and my stomach were happily full.

After finally getting back to my hotel, I called my wife, Susie, and told her of this unbelievable experience. The next morning they picked me up and I was taken around Liege, a lovely city, to visit some of the family's businesses as they had a leather store and boutique shops. They then drove me to the Brussels airport for my flight back home. It was a very touching farewell as we embraced and kissed and cried as we left each other.

A few years later, Susie and I were in Amsterdam and we arranged to go to Liege to visit the family. We encountered the same wonderful hospitality, family, and food! Susie loved the little grandchildren, for whom we brought gifts, and they seemed to really enjoy her enthusiasm as well. On our return to the train

Herb and Susie.

for our departure to Paris, I sat by the window in our coach car, waving to the family. It was such a reflective moment and being a very emotional type of person, I was crying at the thought of finding a long lost family that even my father didn't know. Susie, sitting next to me, put her hand on my arm and smiled. "It's alright to cry," she said, "but let me ask you a question, 'Who the hell were those people?'" She, of course, was kidding, borrowing a line from the Chevy Chase movie *European Vacation*.

Alone, several years ago, I went back to visit them yet again. Every visit bringing more indelible memories. I was recently saddened to find out that both Benjamin and Jeanette have passed away. I still keep in touch with their children and hope to visit them again soon.

On my mother's side we have relatives in Australia. Her parents came from Russia and first lived in London prior to coming to America. They had a young nephew living with them and he came to live in the United States, as well. However, when they arrived in Ellis Island they were all examined by the immigration doctors and he was found to have an eye disease which wouldn't permit him to enter the country. He was sent back to London and later immigrated to Australia, part of the British Commonwealth, where he settled and raised his family.

On my first tour with a group to Australia and New Zealand, we connected with the family, some of whom lived in Sydney and some in Melbourne. It was a wonderful event having dinner at one of their homes and meeting all the members of their family. The memory of entering their home with the front entrance covered by the beautiful Jacaranda tree still sticks with me. We all sat at a long table and were waited on by the younger family members. There were six of us including my mother-in-law Ruby, my aunt Bess, who was the real connection to corresponding with them, and several others from our group.

I made two other trips to Australia in the following years and once again had the pleasure of visiting with them. Finding and then visiting relatives in these foreign places are such very special memories to me. And, astonishingly, preceded Ancestry.com by many years.

Civil-Liberty

In 2012, I teamed up with the University of Cincinnati History Department to offer a Civil War trip in commemoration of the 150th anniversary of the events that tore our nation apart. I met the head of the department, Dr. Christopher Phillips, and we planned and presented our first trip.

I was a graduate from U.C. and my major was American History, so it was really exciting to be part of this inaugural adventure. We advertised the trip and thirty-four excited individuals embarked on what was to be four years of trips to exciting destinations led by Dr. Phillips and myself.

Our first year's trip was to Washington, D.C., where we visited Lincoln's Cottage, a little known place where Lincoln would retreat to escape the hot weather of Washington and historically, where he also drafted the Emancipation Proclamation, abolishing slavery; and, Ford's theatre where President Lincoln was shot. In addition, we visited the battlefields of Antietam, Bull Run, Gettysburg, Fredericksburg, Harpers Ferry, and the Booth Trail which followed the escape route of John Wilkes Booth.

The entire trip was done by motor coach, staying in various hotels along the way and enjoying a variety of meals.

The next year we created Civil War Revisited II, traveling south from Cincinnati to visit both Abraham Lincoln's birthplace and Jefferson Davis's birthplace, both located in Kentucky only sixty miles apart. We continued to Shiloh, Vicksburg, and Montgomery, Alabama, the first capital of the Confederacy; followed by Atlanta, Chattanooga for the Battle of Lookout Mountain, and back to Kentucky before arriving back home. This was a journey of over 1,600 miles.

The third installment, Civil War Revisited III, went to Virginia. Our first stop was in Lexington where we visited the Stonewall Jackson home, the Virginia Military Institute, plus Washington and Lee University. From there we traveled on to Richmond, the Confederate Capital, where we headquartered to visit all of the surrounding battlefields and important sites pertinent to the Civil War. Finally, we ended at Appomattox where Robert E. Lee surrendered to Ulysses S. Grant, ending the war.

The fourth trip focused on the American Revolution. We headed northeast through Pennsylvania, where we visited both Valley Forge and Philadelphia. In Philadelphia we had quite a unique surprise. After a dinner at a historic tavern we were escorted, by a character dressed in 18th century clothing, to Independence Hall, which was closed for the night. After knocking on the door, our guide got us admitted inside where we were entertained by actors assuming the roles of Thomas Jefferson, Benjamin Franklin, and John Adams, debating who would write the Declaration for Independence from Great Britain. It was a highlight of the trip, to be in the sacred hall where the birth of our nation took place.

We continued on to Boston to see where the first battles took place in Lexington and Concord, Bunker Hill, and the homes of Paul Revere and others. Continuing on to upstate New York, we visited Saratoga and Ft. Ticonderoga before returning back home.

These four trips were a labor of love for me. It took hours of research to find the routing; local guides to provide great knowledge at the places we visited; and, the hotels and restaurants along the way, let alone estimating our daily mileage to maximize the historical stops throughout each day. Dr. Phillips filled in the gaps while we were on the motor coach and we also showed themed movies including the Ken Burns Civil War series. In advance, we presented books to all our guests so they could have knowledge of the places we were going to visit. On each of the four trips from 2012–2015, we had about eighty percent repeaters on each trip. The majority were enthusiastic senior adults taking notes, pictures, asking questions, and enjoying seeing each other over these years.

This was a very satisfying experience for me. I told Dr. Phillips that I felt like I wrote a thesis for each of the trips we presented. They will go down in my memory as a creation of historical events revisited which were, happily, enjoyed by so many.

Borscht

Several years ago, we put together a tour for a private group going to Moscow to dedicate a Baptist seminary that was a former day care center for Russian worker's children. I was asked to escort this group of twenty-one persons which would also continue on after our Moscow stop to visit the Golden Ring, a ring of cities that preserve the memory of the most important and significant events in Russian history where you have the famous golden onion-domed churches.

On our first full day in Moscow, we went to the seminary where over one hundred people from all parts of the world came to celebrate the dedication of this wonderful facility. Russia was just emerging from its communist past and allowing religion to once again be allowed openly. This was a wonderful facility with living space for single and married students, computer labs, a magnificent kitchen, dining hall, and other facilities. I met people from all over the world including a gentleman from India who told me he was acquainted with Mother Teresa.

That evening, we assembled in the dining room for a dinner which was served by the students. They mentioned they would be passing a basket for any gift offering we wished to make. I took out a crisp new twenty-dollar bill and had it ready in hand. A speaker got up and announced that he was from the northern Illinois delegation and he had a check to give to the school in the amount of $75,000. With that, I reached into my pocket and took out another twenty dollars. Many more speakers came forward and continued to present extremely large checks to the school. On the way out the door, where the donation basket was placed, I wadded up my two twenty-dollar bills, quickly tossed them into the basket, and speedily exited the room.

While on this trip we stayed at the deluxe Baltschug Kempinski Hotel, the finest in Moscow. I could look out of my room's window and see Lenin's Tomb on Red Square. After a while, the group got tired of eating fancy food and wanted to go to a McDonald's for a hamburger. The twenty-one of us walked about thirty minutes from our hotel to the restaurant, got our Big Mac fix, and started walking back to the hotel. Some in our group were elderly and not doing too well on the walk back. Two of them were really struggling and falling way behind the rest of the group. I stayed with them and we stood on the corner hoping to see a taxi come by. There were none in sight.

Someone had previously told me that if you put out your hand like you were hitchhiking, a private car would likely stop and take you to where you wanted to go. In desperation, I gave it a try. All of a sudden, a car pulled over to the curb. I told the couple to get into the car, told the driver three words in English, "Baltschug Kempinski Hotel," gave him a handful of Russian rubles and off he went with the couple. I said a prayer and hoped they wouldn't end up in Siberia. I continued walking back to our hotel and about fifteen minutes later upon my arrival, I breathed a sigh of relief as the couple was sitting in the lobby amongst the others who had walked back. When they saw me everyone asked, "How did they get here ahead of us?" I answered, "You have witnessed a miracle."

On our continuation through the Golden Ring we stayed at a 50s-style Soviet hotel located on the Volga River. On each floor there was a desk located near the elevator manned by a warden-like woman who demanded your room key every time you left the premises.

One pleasant evening, we all casually went outside near the plaza river bank. Somehow, we all joined together and started singing songs like "You Are My Sunshine" and so on. We soon were joined by folks from other countries such as Brits, French, Italian, and even Russians. It was an exceptional feeling while in a country recently under the thumb of communism.

Showtime

Some of our most popular group trips have been to attend musical events. Our family has always enjoyed popular music whether it was seeing famous personalities perform as solo artists or watching Broadway shows. I think this originates from being with Susie's mother and father who were wonderful entertainers. Our daughter Julie's first theatrical experience was playing Brigitta in the Sycamore High School production of *The Sound of Music* and we probably purchased fifty tickets for each of the performances to give to family and friends.

During our high school days, Susie and I would go with friends to Coney Island and hear her father Barney Rapp and mother Ruby Wright perform at Moonlight Gardens. Later, when I joined the Barney Rapp Agency in 1974, we were booking entertainment and contracted various performers including the talent from the Bob Braun show and others like Boots Randolph and Jeannie C. Riley to perform at various locations. I have many memories from those days and it's remarkable what sticks with you. On one occasion I had Cliff Lash, the conductor and pianist for both the Ruth Lyons and Bob Braun shows, with me in Indianapolis and we were driving back to Cincinnati in a December snow storm when we heard the radio report on the fatalities at The Who concert in Cincinnati. This is one of those occasions where you remember exactly where you were when you heard of a tragic event.

Through the years, we put together many show and concert trips including Celine Dion, Elton John, and Bette Midler at Caesars Palace in Las Vegas; as well as, Barbra Streisand, Barry Manilow, Neil Diamond, Paul Anka, Neil Sedaka, The Four Freshman, Marie and Donny Osmond, Andy Williams, Olivia Newton-John, Tony Bennett, and many others. Plus, we also hosted annual trips to Branson and Nashville.

Our Broadway Show trips to Chicago or New York have always been a favorite. For over thirty years we have arranged tours to see Tony Award winning shows including *Wicked, Kinky Boots, Phantom of the Opera, Les Misérables, The Producers, Fiddler on the Roof, Chicago, A Chorus Line, The Lion King, Hamilton,* and, of course, the annual Radio City Christmas Spectacular featuring the Rockettes. These show trips are combined with dinners at restaurants like Sardi's and city sightseeing to add to the entertaining getaways.

Favorites

I'm constantly asked, out of all the places I have visited, what is my favorite? I pause before answering and then usually answer, "Switzerland," as I love visiting that country; but, then I go on to tell about some of my other journeys as well.

My travels have taken me to many wonderful and exciting destinations: Our visit to Vietnam after it opened to tourism; the excitement of seeing what was left of the Berlin Wall while visiting this reunified city; the thrill of standing on a hill overlooking the ancient biblical city of Jerusalem, the home of Judaism, Christianity, and Islam; the chilling effect of visiting Nazi concentration camps and questioning how humans could be so cruel to other human beings; beholding the beauty of America in our National Parks, magnificent cities, Civil War battlefields, and our country's natural beauty; exploring the exotic places found in China, Singapore, Japan, Thailand, India, and Africa; the splendor of the Down Under countries of Australia and New Zealand; witnessing all the European countries where many native people went on to make America the true melting pot.

Herb with his daughter, Julianne, and son, Steve, in Puerto Rico.

I could go on and on recounting the magnificent locations I have been, but my favorite thing really is the education I received from traveling to so many places. I have enjoyed meeting people from all over the world and learning of their cultures. It has given me a broader perspective and made me a more understanding person. We are all really the same, hoping and fighting for better lives for ourselves and our children. Traveling is the true United Nations of our world.

Many of my travel highlights come from shared tales over delicious food, so I always recall restaurants like The Old Swiss House in Lucerne, Switzerland, for the best schnitzel; Taverna Flavia in Rome; Harry's American Bar in Venice; the Hofbräuhaus in Munich; Virgilio's in St. Thomas; and, so many more that I think about and return to many times.

Then, there are special places to visit such as the Sydney Opera House; Queenstown in New Zealand; Cape Town, South Africa; the rivers of Europe; the Canadian cities of Toronto, Montreal, Quebec, Vancouver, and Victoria and all the Canadian Maritime Provinces; the capital cities of Europe like Vienna, Paris, Berlin, Stockholm, Helsinki, Copenhagen, Prague, Rome, Moscow; cruises to the Caribbean and Europe; and, of course, all of the wonderful places in our beautiful America like Niagara Falls, the Grand Canyon, all our national parks, rivers, museums, cities, towns and villages. There is so much to see, taste, smell, and enjoy.

Jim Scott and his wife, Donna, with Susie and Herb in Vienna.

I thoroughly enjoy cruising, as these fantastic vessels have allowed us to visit so many places in the world. I'm especially fond of river cruises which I was first introduced to on the Rhine River in 1976, before it became so popular for companies to sail on European and Asian rivers; and, of course, our great American rivers like the Mississippi, Ohio, Columbia, Tennessee, and more. These cruises enable us to see so many places in the comfort of sailing on beautiful, modern ships that become our home each time we finish our day of touring.

Rosemary Clooney and Susie Reisenfeld on the *Mississippi Queen*.

Chuckles

I have been known to tell a few jokes while on our trips. After the city tour highlights, between courses of a flavorsome dinner, or during a bus ride back to the hotel following a show, adding a smile or laugh to the day is always something I enjoy. For those who have said they wish they could remember the jokes so they could pass them along, this chapter is for you.

The Bell Ringer

The great bell ringer, Quasimodo of Notre-Dame Cathedral in Paris, had died and the main priest put an ad in the paper looking for a new ringer. One day there was a knock on the door and the priest opened it to see a man standing there without any arms. He said that he should go around to the kitchen for a meal. The man said, "No, I come from a long line of European bell-ringers and I came for the job you advertised." The priest told him he wouldn't be qualified due to his handicap, but the man insisted and ran up the many flights of stairs with the priest in pursuit.

When he reached the top of the tower, he was staring at three large bells, each of a different size. The priest begged the man to

133

come down, but he insisted he had been practicing for this position and he could do it. The priest relented and allowed him to proceed. He stood in front of the smallest bell, closed his eyes, concentrated, and with a swift movement butted his head against the bell and with a bong, his front teeth came flying out. The priest told him to stop, but he uttered he could do it and stepped in front of the next bell and again using his head hit the bell with a thud, which produced a small bong and a terrible gash in his forehead. The priest tried in vain to stop him from going for the third bell. The man sputtering and bleeding, braced himself against the wall and took a flying leap at the last bell, sailed past it and out of the tower window landing ten stories below on the ground, dead.

The priest ran down to the bottom of the tower where a crowd had gathered. The police had arrived and summoned the priest over to the dead bell-ringer. They asked, "Father, do you know this poor man?" The priest thought for a moment and answered, "No, I don't, but his face sure rings a bell!"

Now, several months later, still looking for a bell-ringer, there was a knock on the door and when the priest opened it he saw the same poor fellow without any arms standing in front of him. Before he could say a word, the fellow said, "I'm the identical twin of the fellow who tried before. I'm the last of the European bell-ringers and I have come for the position." The priest told him no way, but he ran past him and up the many flights to the top of the tower, again with the priest in hot pursuit. He stood in front of the first and then the second bell and used his head with the same bad results. Finally he darted through the air at the last bell, out the window, and onto the ground below, dead.

The priest couldn't believe this was happening again, ran down the flights of stairs and out onto the ground level where again a crowd had gathered and the police came up to the priest and asked, "Father, do you know who he is?" The priest answered, "No I don't, but he's a dead ringer for his brother!"

Mistaken Identity

Two men were sitting at opposite ends of a bar counter. One was Jewish and the other Asian. They had their beverages in hand and continued to stare at each other for quite some time. Finally, the Jewish man walked over to the Asian man and punched him, knocking him to the floor. In sheer pain the Asian said, "Why did you hit me?" The Jewish man answered, "That's for bombing Pearl Harbor." The Asian man answered back, "I'm Chinese. That was the Japanese." The Jewish man replied "Chinese, Japanese, it's all the same to me." And returned to his bar stool.

A few minutes later the Asian man walked over to the Jewish man and punched him off of his stool, onto the floor. The Jewish man looked up and said, "Why did you hit me?" The Asian answered, "That's for sinking the Titanic." The Jewish man answered, "The Titanic was sunk by an iceberg." The Asian man answered, "Iceberg, Goldberg, it's all the same to me."

Rumble Room

A young couple went to Chicago for their honeymoon. Not having a lot of money they took a room near the elevated train in downtown Chicago. On their first morning the husband told his wife that he had to make a business call and would be back soon.

Now the young bride wasn't very happy with the room because every time the train would come by, the room would shake and nearly throw them out of bed. So, after her husband left, she called the hotel manager to come up to see the problem first hand and see if they could get a different room.

He came up and told her that he never had a complaint about this room. She told him, "If you don't believe me, lie beside me in the bed and you will see what I mean when the train passes by." He climbed in bed beside her and a minute later the door opened and in walked her husband returning from his call. Seeing the man in bed with his wife, he yelled, "What are you doing in bed with my wife?" The man nervously answered, "I know you won't believe this, but we're waiting for a train."

Mind Boggling

Two men and one wife were standing in the kitchen reminiscing about old times. The wife went over to the stove, making dinner. The two men kept talking and then the subject of fishing came up. The one man said to the other, "Who was that incredible guy we used to go fishing with, the one that could always throw the hook in the water and instantly a fish would bite?" They each thought for a while and couldn't remember the man's name. Suddenly one said to the other, "What's the name of that flower that grows in summer and has thorns?" The other man answered, "A Rose?" The one said, "Thanks," and yelled into the kitchen, "Hey Rose, what's the name of that guy we use to go fishing with?"

The Linguist

A man walks into a pet store and tells the clerk he is looking for a nice pet to be with his mother who lives in Florida. The clerk suggests a nice little puppy, but the man answered that wouldn't do because his mother lives on the 25th floor of her building and she couldn't go out to walk the dog. He next suggests a kitten and again the reply is no; his mother is allergic to cat hair. He next suggests a gerbil and the man answered that she would go crazy hearing that thing spinning the wheel all day in his cage.

Racking his brain, the clerk says, "We have a parrot here that speaks seven languages and would be a great companion for your mother." When he learned that the parrot was $5,000 he hesitated and then finally relented, "OK, I'll take it and please ship it down to my mother." A week later the man called his mother and asked, "Mom, how do you like the bird?" She answered, "It was delicious." He screamed, "Mom, you ate the bird? It spoke seven languages and cost $5,000." She replied, "Well, why didn't it say something?"

How Are Things

A man was on a vacation and called back home to his brother wanting to know how his loving cat was doing. The man replied,

"Oh Charlie, I hate to tell you this but your cat jumped out of the window onto the roof and then fell off and died." The brother cried out, "Why did you have to tell me it happened that way? You could have eased me into it by saying my cat jumped out of the window onto the roof so you called the fire department to get her down. But, the cat jumped out of the fireman's arms and landed in a tree and then fell. You took her to the veterinarian where he fixed her broken leg and she was doing better for a couple of days; but, then she caught an infection and finally peacefully passed away." He continued, "That is the way you should give out bad news, not shocking people." He then asked, "How is Mom doing?" The brother answered, "Well she went up on the roof—!"

Holy Roller

The Pope arrives in New York City's JFK airport and waits for his driver to take him into downtown Manhattan. He waits but the car service never shows up. Finally, he hails a taxi, gets in the backseat and they leave the airport. About a mile into the drive, the Pope tells the driver to pull over to the curb. He tells the driver to get in the back seat and he would take over, as he always wanted to drive a taxi. The driver tells the Pope he can't do that so the Pope asks him if he is Catholic. If he is, the Pope tells him, he is the boss, "so let me drive and you get in the back."

The Pope starts driving, exceeding the speed limit and is stopped by a policeman. When the policeman looks in the cab, he can't believe his eyes, goes back to his car and radios the chief. He said, "Chief, you won't believe the car I just stopped and who is in it!" The chief replied, "Is it the mayor?" The policeman replied "No." "Is it the Governor?" Again, "No." "Is it the President?" Once again, "No!" The chief, frustrated, asked "Well, who is it then?" The policeman replied, "I don't know, but whoever he is, he must be mighty important because the Pope is driving him!"

Not Finished

I hope you have enjoyed reading about some of the many adventures during my forty-three plus years in the travel industry. Only time will tell what interesting experiences the next trip will bring. We have been fortunate to meet thousands of wonderful people along the way, many who have become lifelong friends. These anecdotes are mostly funny and detail the weird things that happened throughout the years. Understandably, there are so many more wonderful stories. Perhaps for another time.

I was blessed to be in this wonderful industry where I traveled the world with my life-partner, my loving wife, Susie, whom we lost in 2015. I miss her so, but my heart is full when I look at our hundreds of pictures from the places we visited together. We were also lucky to share so many of our travels with our son, Steve, who put up a valiant fight against melanoma cancer, the dreaded disease that took his life at a very young age; and, our beautiful and wonderful daughter, Julianne, who is my strength and whose attitude reminds me to try and stay positive in the way she always finds good in people and things.

I want to thank my good friend and associate, Jim Mogan, whom I have been privileged to work with for over forty years. Also, other longtime associates and friends: Joel Pieper, Tammi Smith, Tammy Little, Debbie Crockett, Geri Dunstan, Sharon Lawrence, Anna Mincy, Marylou McCarthy, Denise Gehring, Laura Rinsky, Barbara Herbert, Louella Boyers, Ray Barker and all the others from Barney Rapp and Provident Travel. And, of course, my mother-in-law, Ruby Wright Rapp, who first gave me the opportunity to join her, in 1976, in the creation of a great organization.

Finally, I want to thank all of you that have traveled with me along the way. It has been a privilege being your escort and fellow passenger all of these years. You have been supportive and I consider all of you my friends. I miss so many who are no longer here with us.

Travel opens up unimaginable horizons. We can learn so much from the places we visit, the people we meet, and from those new traveling companions who become our friends. I'm often reminded of the happiness experienced when families enjoy traveling together. We had ours, traveling with Susie, Julianne, and Steve, my in-laws Barney and Ruby, my mother and father, Sarah and Dave, my brother, Sylvan, and my sister-in-law, Beryl, my Aunt Bess, Uncle Danny, Aunt Evelyn, and my sister and brother-in-law's, Patty and Ray Nulsen, Mike and Nancy Farasey, and Cindy and Eric Hoeffel and many of their children. Wonderful memories!

Always remember,
The more you keep checking inn,
the more you get out of life.

About the Author

Herb Reisenfeld is a Cincinnati native who graduated from the then New Woodward High School, the University of Cincinnati, and attended the Salmon P. Chase school of law. He resides with his daughter, Julianne, in Amberley Village, Ohio. He was married to the love of his life, Susie, for fifty-two years prior to her passing in 2015. They also had a son, Steve, who lost his battle to melanoma cancer in 2012.

Herb catches the champagne cork during singing of the "Champagneergalopp" at Strauss concert, Vienna, 2004.

Herb started working on travel promotions for the Dubois Chemical Company's annual employee management trips, where he worked. He later went to work for the Barney Rapp Agency in 1974; and, in 1976, with his mother-in-law, Ruby Wright Rapp, formed Barney Rapp Travel, a full line professional travel agency.

Along with a great staff including Jim Mogan, Barney Rapp became the leading provider of group tours throughout the region. In addition, the agency handled individuals and company incentive programs for television and radio stations, newspapers and other commercial companies.

In 1980, Herb worked with WLW-T personality Bob Braun to operate his annual Hawaiian Island trip which had over 436 participants. This became an annual tour for many years and moved on to include both Europe land and river cruises, as well as, domestic trips. Bob, Herb, Susie, and Wray Jean became very close friends.

The talent-hosted trips continue to this day. Past trips included special guests Nick, Nina, and Rosemary Clooney. Many trips were also hosted by WLW radio personality Jim Scott and his wife Donna. The All-Star Baseball Cruise and Reunion is entering its thirty-third year and features Marty Brennaman, present and past Cincinnati Reds players, managers including the late Sparky Anderson, and the much admired Reds pitcher and broadcaster Joe Nuxhall.

Herb is now in his forty-third year in this wonderful business and looks forward to continuing to travel with the many friends he's met on these trips and to meeting many new ones.

This book recounts incidents that came from his fabulous career as a trip director. Hopefully there will be many more!

Still traveling!